ON THE OTHER SIDE OF THE GARDEN

2nd Edition

By

Virginia Ruth Fugate

Foundation for Biblical Research

Citrus Heights, CA 95610

On the Other Side of the Garden

1st Edition Copyright 1992 by Virginia Fugate
2nd Edition Copyright 2004 by Virginia Fugate

Published by Foundation for Biblical Research
8319 Parkside Lane, Citrus Heights, CA 95610

Printed in the United States of America

ISBN 1-889700-40-1

DEDICATED

to the glory of God the Father and
the Lord Jesus Christ

Psalm 115:1

*Not unto us, O LORD, not unto us, but unto thy
name give glory, for thy mercy, and for thy
truth's sake.*

Romans 11:36

*For of him, and through him, and to him, are all
things: to whom be glory for ever. Amen.*

ACKNOWLEDGEMENTS

How can I give the proper credit to all those who influenced the writing of this book? There have been so many, I am sure to miss someone. I will never forget those who were instrumental in leading me to where I could hear the Gospel of Christ. They surrounded me in 1968 with their witness and their testimonial lives.

I owe a debt of gratitude to Dr. Lowell Wendt, my first pastor, who in 1968 made my need for salvation known. Under his tender teaching I accepted Christ and he baptized most of my family.

Vickie Kraft, an instructor for Child Evangelism Fellowship also stands out as one of the most influential people in my life. As a baby believer, I joined CEF thinking I wanted to teach children. However, I was the one who was taught. I sat mesmerized on the edge of my chair, as God used Vickie to teach me that His love, grace, and provision could be real in my life. I was thirty years old, but I was like a hungry child feeding on His magnificent Word.

God also used several other excellent Bible teachers, including my own dear husband, to teach me. Through their teaching I learned the Word of God and began to realize His will for my life.

Last, but not least, are those who read the very rough draft of this book and gave their excellent suggestions, constructive criticisms, and advice. This novice writer is deeply grateful to all of them for their patient encouragement.

My deepest gratitude, however, is to God and for all that He has created. To Him there can be no repayment; I can offer only my reverence and devotion. My earnest prayer is that this book will honorably represent and glorify the Lord Jesus Christ, my Savior.

FORWARD
To the Second Edition

On the Other Side of the Garden was written for your benefit and to the glory of God. There has been no attempt to manipulate a woman's emotions or to appeal to her vanity in its message. **Only the woman who desires to know the truth and to serve God is likely to complete this book at all.** It is a straight forward, no apology presentation of Biblical truths about God's design for womankind and about the most important human relationship of a woman's life – marriage. Throughout its pages you will also learn a great deal about yourself that will enable you to be more successful in your overall spiritual growth.

After fifteen years of collecting notes on womanhood, my gentle and quiet-spirited wife set aside her fears and insecurities and put her studies in writing the First Edition of, *On the Other Side of the Garden* in 1992. She felt this book was necessary because other Christian books she had read on marriage appeared to either teach the man how to become more effeminate or they centered on a psychological approach for the husband and wife relationship. They often promoted people-managing techniques (or manipulation) to get others to do what is wanted. This seemed to her to be a self-centered motive. Understanding how your husband thinks and, therefore, how to communicate with him better, is a valuable asset in interpersonal relationships. However, humanistic manipulation is not a Christian concept.

Now, thirteen years later, Virginia has completed the Second Edition of this valuable book that has already been used in hundreds of Bible studies for women around the country. This edition is basically the same, uncompromising look at whom is the woman; what is her role; and how she can complement her unique man. Its message is centered solely on what God's Word teaches about the subject. At times it will appear that the information given is one-sided because it does not deal with what a husband should be or do. Instead, this book is for women only. It reveals how a woman can live her life to the glory of God, **even if her husband never does what he is supposed to with his life.**

Not only has my precious wife studied and taught Biblical womanhood, she is a qualified "older woman" with the credentials to teach younger women. In our forty-six years of marriage, she has faithfully lived up to all of the truths presented herein as she learned them. She patiently lived as my helpmate for our first twenty difficult years while I searched for God and my manhood. I know of no other woman of whom I could better testify: "Virginia is truly a Biblical woman who is living successfully in today's world." My prayer for each reader is that you might experience the relationship my wife and I now possess, which is due largely to her having lived most of her life according to the principles set forth in this book.

J. Richard Fugate

Virginia's second book, *Victorious Women* illustrates the principles taught in the first book and cites several real-life examples of changed lives that will encourage even the most faint-hearted woman.

TABLE OF CONTENTS

SECTION ONE - FOUNDATIONS

SECTION TWO - OPPOSITIONS

SECTION THREE - APPLICATIONS

INTRODUCTION TO THE 2ND EDITION

The first edition of *On the Other Side of the Garden* was printed in 1992. I dedicated it to God and prayed that He would take my offering and use it to His glory. It was my prayer that the book would free women from the slavery of humanistic feminism. My deepest desire was for the readers to see God's truth and praise Him for the beauty of their created design.

Since that time, numerous women have written to tell me "God has changed my life!" Over and over again, they would glorify God for His Divine Word and plan rather than praise me for my human words. These women viewed me as only a human instrument used by God, not as a celebrity to be mimicked. For this I praise Him. He has answered my prayer that I would be minimized and that He would be glorified.

He must increase, but I must decrease (John 3:30).

Since 1992, many women have told me that *On the Other Side of the Garden* helped them understand Biblical womanhood for the first time. As these women applied God's truths in their marriages they experienced the joy of seeing His power work in their lives and they were elated. However, along with the life changing joy they experienced, some women also became painfully aware of their past failures. Things they had said and done were etched deeply into their consciences. As these women faced their past, they felt deeply saddened and questioned whether their lives could ever be repaired. **If, at any time** you begin to feel despondent over your own past, please turn immediately to **Chapter XXIV, Help! I Have Done Everything Wrong** before reading further. This chapter will help you realize that you are not alone. Everyone falls short of God's perfection.

For all have sinned, and come short of the glory
of God (Romans 3:23).

Chapter XXIV will help you to put your past behind you and to move forward into your future. Our God is a God of restoration and peace. In Him we can learn from our previous mistakes, but we need not allow those failures or sins to prevent us from experiencing a successful future. By His power and grace we can reach "the high calling of God in Christ Jesus!"

> *... but this one thing I do, forgetting those things which are behind, and reaching forth unto those things which are before, I press toward the mark for the prize of the high calling of God in Christ Jesus* (Philippians 3:13b-14).

May God abundantly bless you as you live Biblical womanhood.

Virginia Fugate
May, 2004

INTRODUCTION TO THE 1ST EDITION

A Christian woman today faces a more difficult task living her life according to Biblical teachings than at any other time in history. Magazines, television programs, billboards, textbooks, movies, and newspapers all contain information that in one way or another debases the Biblical role of the woman. These influences are so dominant that even the Christian woman often forms her attitudes and opinions from human sources, rather than basing them on God's Word. Without the knowledge of God's Word, a woman has nothing but the opinions of others and her own feelings to help her discern these false teachings.

Furthermore, there is an even wider variance in the level of understanding of and commitment to Biblical womanhood among Christian women today. This variance is proof that anti-Biblical sources of information have successfully influenced, and confused, many Christian women.

Some Christian women truly do attempt to live their lives in accordance with God's will. However, a large number have been influenced into accepting a viewpoint that combines Christian standards with whatever is the current popular opinion. Such women live suspended awkwardly somewhere between Biblical womanhood and conformity with the world. Other Christian women have abandoned the Biblical model entirely. These women's lives and marriages are indistinguishable from the unbelieving world.

On the Other Side of the Garden was written from a Biblical prospective and is meant to offset the predominantly humanistic information that women see and hear about womanhood today. The purpose of this book is to provide Biblical insight to all Christian women about the importance of Biblical womanhood. It is my hope that God will use what I have written to foster a renewed commitment to His Word and to encourage Christian women to live their lives as testimonies to the correctness of God's design.

On the Other Side of the Garden is divided into three sections:

Section I, Foundations, is the establishment of the principles of Biblical womanhood from God's perspective. God created the woman and "designed" her for a specific purpose. The terms, "God's design for womanhood," or "womanhood's design," used extensively throughout this book, refer to more than just the woman's role as wife, mother, and homemaker. They refer to the purpose of God for the woman in every area of her life including her uniqueness, her importance, her privileges, and her responsibilities. **Foundations** form the premise on which the following two sections are based.

Section II, Oppositions to Biblical Womanhood, alerts Christian women to the anti-Biblical position of the past fifty or more years of consistent attack against Biblical womanhood. Satan's subtle deceptions are so masterful that women who desire autonomy have been easy prey for his conquest. This section will help to identify the types of lies that lead women away from their Biblical roles.

Section III, Applications for Practical Living, expounds on the Biblical foundations presented in **Section I** and applies them to real life. I have personally practiced these principles in my own life and have observed them in the lives of those close to me. I have made many of the mistakes that I am now warning you about and I have learned some of what I know the hard way. I have fallen into pits of despair that you could easily avoid by following God's design. Although experience may be the best teacher, it is also the harshest teacher in terms of heartache and stress. Learning the material in this section could help you avoid some of those heartaches. It could also help you climb out of your own pits of despair and to correct errors in which you are already involved. The practical applications given will lead you to where you can receive the blessings that God promises to those who live according to His design. These blessings are readily available to those who apply the principles of Biblical womanhood to their lives.

My Prayer

My fervent prayer is for each woman who reads this book. May she be refreshed, encouraged, and stimulated to a renewed eagerness in God's truths. May the results of her hearing and obeying God be a heightened sense of His presence in her life, a reinvigorated marriage, and a strengthened family. For these things may she give honor and praise to God alone. I pray further that her life will present to the world a praiseworthy model of God's design for womanhood and that others will be drawn by her example. This prayer is offered in Jesus' name and for His glory.

Virginia Fugate 1992

SECTION I

FOUNDATIONS

CHAPTER I

WHATEVER HAPPENED TO OLD-FASHIONED LOVE?

The lyrics of a once-popular song began with the words, "Whatever happened to old-fashioned love?" In this song the singer yearned for a love that would see him through the good and the bad times; the kind of love that would last into old age – a love like his grandparents enjoyed. Occasionally, I still hear that song and my heart aches for all the modern couples who long for, but do not experience, an "old-fashioned love."

Why is old-fashioned love so rare in our marriages today? Perhaps, it is because most couples expect the immature, emotional attraction they originally felt for one another to carry their marriages forever. People have come to believe that true love is romantic and magical – a dreamy, head-in-the-clouds type of infatuation. After a few years of marriage they often suffer extreme disappointment when they discover that the "magic" is gone and what is left are problems and children.

Modern men and women seem totally unaware that a loving marriage, like any other worthwhile endeavor in life, requires an unwavering commitment and sacrificial effort to thrive. They are oblivious to the fact that what their grandparents' had was strength of character – the integrity to honor their commitments no matter what. Our grandparents knew that loving another person meant wanting and doing what is best for the loved one, not demanding what one wants for oneself. Sadly, many people today have discarded the concept of old-fashioned love and traded it for something superficial and valueless. They give up on developing the oneness of marriage and replace it with the singleness of self-interest. They discard commitment and make self-gratification the criteria for determining life's choices. Demanding autonomy, they have placed self above all others and even argue they have the "right" to do so. They are looking for fulfillment without commitment to anyone else (including God), but they will not find it; they might as well be looking for an ice cube on the sun.

People often get married simply because they are physically and/or emotionally attracted to one another. However, a marriage based on attraction alone is superficial and insecure. If a couples' initial attraction does not mature into a deeper attachment, it will soon fade away. This "attachment phase" is the result of an unshakeable loyalty to one another that remains long after the physical/emotional attraction settles into a routine. There are no human words that can adequately describe the security a woman can have in the attachment phase of love. But, knowing such a love myself, I will try.

The "attachment phase" is based on two people blending into oneness of thought and existence. Such oneness can only be developed over a long period of time. In this stage the words "I," "me," and "mine" are replaced with "we," "us," and "ours." Considering the other's needs to be more important than one's own becomes natural and effortless because each partner operates as one, not as two independent entities. This "attachment phase" is the very core of the old-fashioned love for which every married woman longs.

There is no substitute for the companionship and compatibility between two people who have shared years of experiences: the same people, places, music, and events. Couples who have nurtured children together have memories that continue long after the children are grown. Warm memories, such as how they laughed when their first child said she had "pilty peet" (filthy feet) after playing in the mud, continues to unite them as they use this phrase themselves while gardening. In the attachment stage of love, a couple is so united that each member often knows without a word being spoken, what the other is feeling, thinking, wanting, or needing. They can even finish each other's sentences.

Nothing bonds a couple together like living through illnesses and family crises. There is no love like the love that has been tested to its very limits and has grown stronger as a result. Love becomes more meaningful to those who have lived through heartbreaks that seemed as if they would never mend, yet somehow always did.

Unwavering commitment is the glue that binds a married couple together through all the ups and downs of life. Such commitment develops the kind of love that cannot be torn apart. It is a selfless, charitable, and sacrificial gift rather than a self-centered demand to receive. The reward for those who work at developing this attachment stage is a deepened love that is worth any pain or effort to acquire.

After all the years of overcoming trials together, it is wonderful to hear him declare his love for you daily. It is delightful to kiss the bald spot on the top of his head and for him to see past your "laugh lines" and tell you he actually likes your gray hair. It is comforting to grow older together and experience a love that continues growing day by day.

The best of times begin only after the self-centered motivations of youth are replaced with a love for the other that is greater than the love for oneself. Peace reigns in a mature love because all the battles have been won and the questions have been answered about the give and take of your relationship. It is reassuring to know that together you flow like a two-person canoe on a gentle stream, both paddling in the same direction. There is such immeasurable security in knowing that if you hit rapids, the experience of rowing as one will continue to carry you to safety.

Can a Christian woman live a Biblical life and experience old-fashioned love in this modern world? Not only can she, but the people she loves are depending on her to do just that. Her husband needs her as a Biblical wife and her children learn through her example.

> *Her children arise up, and call her blessed; her husband also, and he praiseth her. Many daughters have done virtuously, but thou excellest them all. Favour is deceitful, and beauty is vain: but a woman that feareth the LORD, she shall be praised* (Proverbs 31:28-30).

This and future generations desperately need Christian women whose lives reflect God's truths – women who trust Him enough to live by His precepts.

> *That ye may be blameless and harmless, the sons of God, without rebuke, in the midst of a crooked and perverse nation, among whom ye shine as lights in the world; Holding forth the word of life* . . . (Philippians 2:15-16a).

As you read this book you will probably experience various emotional reactions. At times you will be filled with inspiration over the purity of God's Word. At other times you will agonize over the difficulty of your everyday reality. But, just as there is happiness in the "attachment stage" of human love, there is also immeasurable joy from, "holding forth the word of life."

I pray that God will use this book to lift you above the pressures of today and that you will come to know the satisfaction that results from a lifetime of living Biblical womanhood.

CHAPTER II

CREATED FOR A PURPOSE

"Who am I? Why am I here?" Every intelligent woman will consider these questions at some point in her life. She realizes that without the correct answers her life could be spent in vain. This is especially true for the Christian woman who desires to live a godly life. Can a woman actually know her true identity? Can she possess complete confidence that she is living her life for a worthwhile purpose? Yes, the Bible says she can!

Understanding God's master plan is necessary in order to answer a woman's questions about life. To answer the question "Who am I?" it is first essential to understand God's pattern, or original blueprint, of the woman. To answer the question, "Why am I here?" we must discover God's purpose in His design for the woman.

What source provides more accurate information about the design and purpose of a creation than the manual written by the original designer? The Bible is just such a manual. With complete accuracy, God's word tells us why the woman was created and defines her purpose and function within God's plan for the benefit of His creation, mankind. The first section of this book is dedicated to revealing God's blueprint for the woman and His designed purpose for giving her life. When a woman functions according to God's design, she is able to have fulfillment in her marriage, success in the training of her children, and confidence in her relationship with God and others.

God's Purposes for the Creation of Mankind

Originally, mankind was perfect as was all of God's creation. God had a specific purpose for each of His creation that went beyond its mere existence. For instance, one of His purposes for mankind was to have productive work, as demonstrated in Genesis 2:15 *And the LORD God took the man, and put him into the garden of Eden to dress it and to keep it.*

God did not leave man without clear instructions as to what He expected of Him. He communicated with Adam, because He intended that mankind should know and obey His Word. He also established His authority over mankind with precise instructions that carried specific consequences for disobedience. Adam was told that he might freely eat of every tree in the garden, *But of the tree of the knowledge of good and evil, thou shalt not eat of it: for in the day that thou eatest thereof thou shalt surely die* (Genesis 2:17).

Adam had all he needed to exist and was unaware of any incompleteness or loneliness until God brought it to his attention. God, not Adam, said, in Genesis 2:18b . . . *it is not good that the man should be alone; I will make him an help fit for him.* God used a parade of creatures to prepare Adam for the presentation of a helper appropriate for him.

> *And out of the ground the Lord God formed every beast of the field, and every fowl of the air; and brought them unto Adam to see what he would call them...* (Genesis 2:19a).

Apparently, both male and female creatures were brought before Adam; because it was during this parade of tangible evidence that Adam noticed he was alone.

> *And Adam gave names to all cattle, and to the*
> *fowl of the air, and to every beast of the field;*
> *but for Adam there was not found an help fit for*
> *him* (Genesis 2:20).

Who Am I?

The woman as a separate entity was not created at the same time, or in the same way, as was the original creation of mankind.

> *And the rib, which the LORD God had taken*
> *from the man, made he a woman, and brought*
> *her unto the man* (Genesis 2:22).

The Bible does not state that God manufactured the woman from the raw materials of the earth as He did the original body of mankind. Instead, God took a rib directly out of His first creation man and molded a woman. This does not mean that woman was an afterthought of God, for her essence was determined from the beginning as an integral part of the species called mankind.

> *So God created man in His own image, in the*
> *image of God created he him; male and female*
> *created he them* (Genesis 1:27).

God molded a second human body around Adam's rib. The original creation of mankind was now in two distinct entities – man and woman. Mankind was no longer the whole, complete creation that it was in the beginning. Two separate entities now existed, each needing the other to make mankind whole.

> *Therefore shall a man leave his father and his*
> *mother, and shall cleave unto his wife: and they*
> *shall be one flesh* (Genesis 2:24).

> *Male and female created he them; and blessed*
> *them, and called their name Adam, in the day*
> *when they were created* (Genesis 5:2).

The man and woman were created to act as a couple. This helps to explain the mystery of marriage: the joining of the two parts into one flesh. This joining does not only refer to the physical union of a man and woman, but to their soul union as well. Men have been writing poems and songs for thousands of years that have spoken of a partial soul uniting between a normal (unscarred by promiscuity) man and woman whenever they begin to have intimate contact. (See also *Song of Solomon*.) After physical intercourse, their souls are even more intertwined, especially that of the woman's with the man's. Any separation afterward cannot be done without soul damage to both; it is as if that which had become one is violently ripped apart.

> *Have ye not read, that he which made them at*
> *the beginning made them male and female, And*
> *said, For this cause shall a man leave father*
> *and mother, and shall cleave to his wife: and*
> *they twain shall be one flesh? Wherefore they*
> *are no more twain, but one flesh. What therefore*
> *God hath joined together, let not man put*
> *asunder* (Matthew 19:4-6). (This important
> message is also recorded in Genesis 2:24 and
> repeated in Ephesians 5:31.)

What Is Woman's Purpose?
Or, Why Am I Here?

God's purpose in forming the woman was to provide for man a mate corresponding to him. God had taken from the male all that was necessary to form "a help meet for him" (a counterpart to the male – a female). He returned to the man, in marriage, that which was taken from him – the woman.

The man was not unaware of the origin of the woman. His first response to seeing her indicates his recognition of her source.

And Adam said, This is now bone of my bones,
and flesh of my flesh; ...(Genesis 2:23a).

Adam had named the creatures of earth, so it was natural for him to give a name to the female – one that would match her purpose for being. Original creation had one generic name, Adam or mankind, but now there were two bodies and two names. Man was now distinctly male, and woman was distinctly female. The Hebrew word for "man" is *Ish*, and the Hebrew word for "woman" is *Isha* (meaning "out of *Ish*").

And Adam said,...she shall be called Woman,
(Isha)*, because she was taken out of Man* (Ish)
(Genesis 2:23).

Even before the Isha was brought forth out of Ish, God stated the woman's purpose. He had said that it was not good for man to be alone. The man needed a companion and a helper suitable for him. The naming of Isha reveals Adam's recognition of the woman as a counterpart of himself, and it indicates that he understood her purpose in functioning as his helpmate.

That the woman was the second entity of the species, mankind, to appear does not make her second best, merely incomplete by herself. By forming the woman *from* Adam, and by bringing her *to* him, God stressed the woman's dependence on, fulfillment in, and relationship to her man.

For the man is not of the woman, but the woman
of the man. Neither was the man created for the
woman, but the woman for the man
(1 Corinthians 11:8-9).

God designed the woman for the man's benefit (Genesis 2:18-20), and out from him (Genesis 2:22-23), and for him (1 Corinthians 11:8-9). There is no indication anywhere in Scripture that a married woman is to have a purpose of her own, apart from her husband. (See the Appendix, Women Alone for comments on the single woman.)

What Does Helper Mean?

The scriptural definition of "helper" is not greatly different from a dictionary definition: "a person or thing that helps or gives assistance, support, etc." Synonyms of helper include: "aide, assistant, supporter, backer, auxiliary." The verb "to help" is defined: "To contribute strength or means to; render assistance to; cooperate effectively with; aid, assist: as in, 'he helped with my work'." [1] These definitions indicate that the woman as a helper is an assistant – the one who helps to achieve the goals of the one leading. His goals become her goals. She cooperatively and effectively assists and renders aid in order to strengthen the man for his own tasks.

A woman has important work to do in order to fulfill her God-given purpose. She should use her intelligence, talents, and abilities in such a way that her efforts give support and encouragement to her man. This could range from providing a stable, comfortable home, to working in her husband's business or giving moral support for his ministry. In other words, she helps her husband in whatever capacity he most needs her assistance.

Scripture never indicates that the woman is lacking in intelligence or abilities. In fact, in order for her to be able to accomplish her tasks, God provides certain excellent abilities that appear mainly to be feminine characteristics. Women (when untainted by sin) tend to be compassionate, understanding, patient, tenacious, and unselfishly nurturing of others.

The woman obviously must have ability, or she would be of no help at all – she would be a hindrance. When a woman accepts her helpmate role, God uses her abilities to aid and complement her husband's role and calling in life. However, the woman who rejects her position as helper is an obstacle to her husband's role; no matter how humanly intelligent or talented she may be. Such a woman renounces her own purpose within God's creation and utilizes her talents in opposition to God's purposes. As a result she can become an obstruction over which her husband must rise in order to reach God's desired objectives. And, he must do it alone, without a helpmate.

Some modern women reject God's design because they mistakenly believe that His purpose for them as helpers is lowly in position and importance. They confuse submissiveness with inferiority and think that the title of "helper" is demeaning. Perhaps these women have never fully analyzed their thoughts in light of God's Word. How could any of God's intended purposes for His creation be demeaning? All that God created deserves exaltation, including His purpose for both man and woman. The woman who lives according to God's perfect design is not degraded; instead, she reflects the beauty of original creation and fulfills the purpose for which she was born. This is the woman who can confidently answer the question, "Who am I?" Also, she is able humbly and graciously to submit to God's answer to the question, "Why am I here?"

CHAPTER III

THE DECEPTION

The woman was designed by God to function in the supportive role of helpmate to her husband. It was God's plan for husband and wife to operate as one, as a single harmonious creation. Nearly every woman desires (even longs for) such a joining of her soul with her man. Why, then, does it appear to be so difficult to achieve compatibility and oneness in marriage today? What has happened to God's original design and purpose for mankind?

To answer these questions we must return to the time of original creation. In the very beginning, Satan challenged God's right to rule over him.

> For thou (Satan) *hast said in thine heart, I will ascend into heaven, I will exalt my throne above the stars of God: I will sit also upon the mount of the congregation, in the sides of the north: I will ascend above the heights of the clouds; I will be like the most High* (Isaiah 14:13-14) (Comment added)

This emphatic statement of rebellion was a rejection of God's rule, as well as Satan's declaration of war against God. Accordingly, everything he has done since this proclamation has been a perpetuation of this revolt. Satan's plot to entice mankind to join his rebellion began when he possessed the serpent and approached the woman in the Garden of Eden.

> *Now the serpent was more subtle than any beast*
> *of the field which the Lord God had made. And*
> *he said unto the woman, Yea, hath God said, Ye*
> *shall not eat of **every** (false) tree of the garden?*
> (Genesis 3:1). (Comment and emphasis added.)

Examine God's original instruction below and compare it to Satan's subtle alteration of God's words in the passage above, indicated by the emphases in both quotations. Observe how Satan asked a slanted question, distorting God's true command in order to make it seem unfair.

> *And the Lord God commanded the man, saying,*
> ***Of every tree of the garden thou mayest freely***
> ***eat:*** *But of the tree of the knowledge of good*
> *and evil, thou shalt not eat of it: for in the day*
> *that thou eatest thereof thou shalt surely die*
> (Genesis 2:16-17). (Emphasis added.)

Satan led the way in the use of subtle alterations of God's Word in order to corrupt its meaning and deny its original purpose. The woman followed Satan's lead with her own seemingly minor modification of God's words.

> *And the woman said unto the serpent, We may*
> *eat of the fruit of the trees of the garden: But*
> *of the fruit of the tree which is in the midst of*
> *the garden, God hath said, Ye shall not eat of*
> *it,* (accurate so far) ***neither shall ye touch it,***
> (a little dramatic embellishment added) *lest ye*
> *die* (accurate again) (Genesis 3:2-3). (Comments
> and emphasis added.)

By modifying God's words the woman revealed that she could be easily led astray. The stage now set, the serpent delivered his mortal thrust.

> *And the serpent said unto the woman, Ye shall*
> *not surely die: For God doth know that in the*
> *day ye eat thereof, then your eyes shall be*
> *opened, and ye shall be as gods, knowing good*
> *and evil* (Genesis 3:4-5). (This is a lie! God had
> clearly communicated in Genesis 2:17 that the
> result would be death.)

Satan insinuated that God was deliberately withholding
something of value from the woman. He implied that she was
being deprived and could obtain, without penalty, that which
God denied her. He suggested that she was merely lacking that
knowledge which would make her **like** a god. Satan's sly
intention was to lead the woman into disobedience by the same
proud and rebellious route he himself had taken. In his evil
rebellion, he had said, *"I will be like the most high."* Notice the
parallel in his offer of superior knowledge to the woman, *"…*
*your eyes **will** be opened, and you will be as gods"*
(Genesis 3:5b). (Emphasis added.)

Finally, convinced by Satan's smooth lies and distortions
of God's Word, the woman took the fatal step – she acted in
opposition to God's stated will.

> *And when the woman saw that the tree was good*
> *for food, and that it was pleasant to the eyes,*
> *and a tree to be desired to make one wise, she*
> *took of the fruit thereof, and did eat, and gave*
> *also unto her husband with her; and he did eat*
> (Genesis 3:6).

By eating the fruit the woman was, in a sense, doing what
was natural for the woman – following leadership. But she did
not follow the leadership of the Lord, nor did she even follow
her husband. Instead, she followed the leadership of a seducer.
The woman's fall into Satan's trap revealed her weakest and
most vulnerable areas of temptation – an intense desire for
knowledge and for self-rule. Even today, the easiest way to

deceive a woman is to appeal to her lust for superior knowledge, or to tempt her with an offer of autonomy.

> *And Adam was not deceived, but the woman*
> *being deceived was in the transgression*
> (1 Timothy 2:14).

Although the woman was deceived, the man was not. The woman had such a powerful influence on the man that she was able to tempt him to choose, **knowingly and willingly**, to disobey God. When Adam followed Eve's lead he revealed his weakest and most vulnerable area of temptation – desire for the woman. The woman's influence is so strong that a man will even abandon his own principles to follow her into sin against God. (Warning: as wives we should exercise great caution in how we influence our husbands.)

When the woman offered the fruit to the man, she stepped outside her designed role and purpose of helpmate. She acted, instead, as the leader. Similarly, when the man accepted the fruit from her hand, he rejected his designed purpose of headship and acted as a follower. These seemingly simple acts reversed the leadership and helpmate positions and corrupted God's perfect design for the relationship of husband and wife. The "battle of the sexes," or which-sex-will-lead and which-will-follow, was born.

The success of Satan's scheme provided him with his most powerful weapon against the human race – knowledge of both the man's and the woman's weaknesses. To this day, he uses this knowledge to lure men and women into straying from God's plan and purpose for their lives.

Satan Still Deceives the Woman Today

Satan continues to wage his war against God today by using mankind as tools. He still attempts to deceive the woman with half-truths and lies fabricated to promote unrest and dissatisfaction.

> *For of this sort are they which creep into houses,*
> *and lead captive silly women laden with sins,*
> *led away with divers lusts, Ever learning, and*
> *never able to come to the knowledge of the truth*
> (2 Timothy 3:6-7).

With insidious distortions similar to those that deceived Eve, the modern woman is subtly influenced today:

"Women who hold to God's design for womanhood are old-fashioned, helpless, self-deprecating, and pathetic. God's design does not protect you; it actually harms you. It holds you back from personal development and denies you the right of self-expression."

And, "You should be in control of your own life. You are an intelligent person. You do not need a man to tell you what to do, especially if he is inferior in intelligence or maturity. Women can do anything as well as, or perhaps even better than, most men. In fact, a woman's solutions to life's problems are often superior to a man's. Men just hold you back from your true potential and greatness."

And also, "Education about women's rights will give you the knowledge and backbone to fight for your freedom. Knowledge equals freedom, the freedom to be your own authority." (Perhaps... to be like gods?)

Women today are assaulted from all sides with a barrage of flattering appeals that are aimed with great precision at their weakest points – especially their intense desire for autonomy. Enticements such as those above continue to promote in women unrest and dissatisfaction with their created purpose. They encourage the woman to wrest from God His right to designate her purpose, and to take for herself total control over her own destiny. Those who promote these false teachings tell the woman that she will benefit by overthrowing male leadership (which ultimately overthrows God's design). They imply that the woman who does not rebel against male leadership is ignorant, or that she is weak and bullied into compliance. They deny that there are any negative consequences for pursuing a course of action that directly opposes God's will.

One vehicle through which Satan promotes his rebellion today is the women's liberation movement. The feminist movement appeals to the woman's desire for autonomy and deliberately promotes the reversal of God's intended order for mankind. The crusaders within this movement are the same as offering modern woman a "forbidden fruit" in order to entice her to rebel against God. Their satanically inspired philosophy has saturated the entertainment world, and all other forms of media, with its almost universal portrayal of the independent woman – happy, fulfilled, and knowledgeable. She is pictured as a woman successfully pursuing an important career, while just as successfully nurturing and leading, a family – often while compensating for the deficiencies of a weak man.

Satan is masterful at manipulating the unwise to join his cause against God's plan for mankind. Camouflaging his contradictions with elegant language and just enough truth to make it plausible, his false philosophy has infiltrated the news media with its cries of "sexism." Meanwhile, government at all levels has responded with laws for "women's rights."

Modern women are constantly bombarded with Satan's false philosophy. They are exposed to feminist propaganda every day through television programs, newspaper reports, and magazine articles. Even those women who do not consciously embrace the rabidly radical positions of the women's liberation movement are, however, still affected by this continuous flow of propaganda. The repetition of the tenets of feminism causes such falsehoods to appear valid by their very familiarity. Evidence of this insidious influence is found even in the church, where fewer and fewer women are living their lives as Biblical helpmates. Those young Christian women who *do* dare to put husband and family first are frequently made to feel inadequate and inferior, somehow guilty of "wasting" their unrealized potential.

In Conclusion

From the beginning of his contact with mankind, Satan has always been secretive and conspiratorial. He knows he cannot overthrow God alone – he apparently intends to continue to use mankind as weapons in his war against the Creator. When the evil one approached the woman in the Garden of Eden, he did not do it in a forthright manner. His tactic was deceptive then and he continues to use the same techniques today. By appealing first to the woman's pride, he was able to deceive her into disobeying God's command. Similarly, the modern woman's pride makes her vulnerable to the misleading tactics of Satan. Because women have an insatiable thirst for self-rule, they too often forsake God's original purpose for their lives and attempt to be their own authority. By acting autonomously, they believe themselves to be following no one's lead but their own. In actuality, they become supporters of Satan's rebellion, followers of his leadership, and unwitting partners with him in his war against God.

I believe the majority of women who are influenced by Satan's present-day deceptions are completely unaware that they are pursuing his pattern of rebellion or that they are being used in his attempt to overthrow God. Ultimately, he will not win, but it is still horrific for any woman to be used as a tool in his evil plot. It is my prayer that thousands of Christian women will choose to radiate the beauty of their created purpose and in so doing be instrumental in exposing Satan's treason.

CHAPTER IV

CURSING TURNED TO BLESSING

The first man and woman were blessed by living in the garden, but they were also warned that there would be consequences if they ate of the tree of the knowledge of good and evil. They did not take God's warning seriously and their disobedience is recorded in Genesis as mankind's first act of sin.

God judged Adam and Eve's disobedience and sentenced them to specific penalties, which they and all their unborn children would bear throughout time. In this chapter we will look at these penalties and at their repercussions on the modern woman. We will also discover how God provided ways to bless the Biblical woman even though she must live with the consequences of mankind's original sin.

The Two Curses

When God judged the sin of the first woman, He pronounced a sentence that contained two penalties. The first penalty concerned her role in childbearing, and the second restated the already established pattern for her relationship with her husband.

*Unto the woman he said, I will greatly multiply
thy sorrow and thy conception; in sorrow thou
shalt bring forth children; and thy desire shall
be to thy husband, and he shall rule over thee*
(Genesis 3:16).

The first penalty that must be borne by women is the pain
associated with the process of childbirth. Not only is childbirth
painful but also, a woman's whole reproductive system often
causes her problems. The menstrual cycle is often more than
just bothersome, and for many women it is a severe monthly
trauma. Even the cessation of the menstrual cycle (menopause)
is difficult for older women. Pregnancy also includes suffering,
from morning sickness and mood swings to backaches and
unwanted weight gain. Finally, the process before delivery is
aptly called "labor."

To focus only on the punishment side of this curse, however,
is to forget that God's purpose for such proclamations is to
draw mankind to Himself. The Bible records at least seventy-
seven times that God placed curses on mankind so that, "*thou
mayest know that I am the Lord.*" The pain in childbirth is not
meant solely to punish, but also to teach. The pain and sorrow
associated with childbirth is a reminder of the results of sin and
the consequences of disobeying God.

The second penalty for the women's sin is twofold: her
desire for her husband, and the principle that a woman is to be
ruled by her husband. Does this really mean what it appears to
mean? Raymond C. Ortlund, Jr. in the book, *Recovering
Biblical Manhood & Womanhood,* has done extensive research
on the Hebrew word translate "desire" in Genesis 3:16b.[2] He
has determined that the meaning of this word conveys a very
strong urge for control. This same word is used in Genesis
4:7b where Cain is told that sin desires to control him, but
instead, that he must rule over sin. Genesis 3:16b might be
more easily understood as follows: You (woman) will "desire

to control" your husband, but he will "rule" (have dominion, reign, have power) over you. A wife is cursed with being ruled by her husband while at the same time she has a strong urge to control him! The woman's "desire" is a weighty sentence indeed. Her urge to control her husband may be as strong as the pull of sin was on Cain.

Because of the woman's desire to control, God's words *"...and he shall rule over thee,"* bring gritting and gnashing of teeth to even naturally compliant women. No woman wants someone else to have power over her. Obviously, these duel drives are the source of the battle-of-the-sexes. While the husband's responsibility before God is to rule his wife, she desires to control him. Without God's grace there would be little hope for any marriage.

The Blessings

It is God's deepest desire to bless mankind (1 Timothy 2:3-4 and John 3:17). Therefore, whenever it is necessary for God's righteousness to judge for disobedience, His love also provides a way to turn any punishment into blessing. Even the judgment on the first woman's original sin can led to one of our greatest benefits. However, to obtain these benefits, it is necessary to understand God's provision for blessing within the penalty. Otherwise, the penalties remain cursing, while the benefits lay dormant and unclaimed.

The First Benefit

Let us look at the first benefit contained within the judgment of the woman's sin. As we have seen, the birth of each child has with it a painful reminder of the result of sin. But with the pain, God also provided the blessing of a new human life. Before the birth of Christ, each new life was a reminder of the hope for the future birth of the promised Savior (Genesis 3:15b). However, since His birth, mankind has been provided the way to a restored relationship with God.

> *But God commendeth his love toward us, in that, while we were yet sinners, Christ died for us. Much more then, being now justified by his blood, we shall be saved from wrath through him. For if, when we were enemies, we were reconciled to God by the death of his Son, much more, being reconciled, we shall be saved by his life. And not only so, but we also joy in God through our Lord Jesus Christ, by whom we have now received the atonement* (Romans 5:8-11).

Today, the pain of childbirth still offers the blessing of a new life to a woman. Most women consider this pain to be a small price to pay when they finally hold their newborn infant. Although we no longer look forward to the birth of a Savior, each newborn can be a blessed reminder that God fulfilled His promise to send mankind a Savior. Let us stop and reflect on how God turned the terrifying curse of death into an extraordinary blessing of eternal life.

1. In Genesis 2:16-17 God "*commanded the man, saying, **Of every tree of the garden thou mayest freely eat:** But of the tree of the knowledge of good and evil, thou shalt not eat of it: for in the day that thou eatest thereof thou shalt surely **die**.*" (Emphasis added.)

2. God cannot lie or act in a way that would violate His character: "*In hope of eternal life, which God, that cannot lie, promised before the world began*" (Titus 1:2). Therefore, the consequences for disobedience of His command, "*thou shalt not eat*," **did** occur. Adam and Eve immediately died spiritually *and* began the process of

physical death at the point of their disobedience. All of future mankind was also condemned to these same deaths.
> *Wherefore, as by one man sin entered into the world, and death by sin; and so death passed upon all men, for that all have sinned:* (Romans 5:12).

3. God's character of righteousness required Him to be true to His word. However, God's character also includes love. *"And we have known and believed the love that God hath to us. God is love"* (1 John 4:16a). It is impossible for Him to act in a way that is not compatible with the integrity of His entire character. Our loving Heavenly Father, who also demands righteousness, turned cursing to blessing when He provided a way for mankind to be restored to Himself.
> *For if by one man's offence death reigned by one; much more they which receive abundance of grace and of the gift of righteousness shall reign in life by one, Jesus Christ. Therefore as by the offence of one judgment came upon all men to condemnation; even so by the righteousness of one the free gift came upon all men unto justification of life. For as by one man's disobedience many were made sinners, so by the obedience of one shall many be made righteous* (Romans 5:17-19).

4. Through the sacrifice of Jesus Christ, the terrifying curse of eternal separation from God has been conquered. The glorious blessing of eternal life is now available to all those who *...believe that Jesus is the Christ, the Son of God* (John 20:31b).
> *But for us also, to whom it shall be imputed, if we believe on him that raised up Jesus our Lord*

> *from the dead; Who was delivered for our*
> *offences, and was raised again for our*
> *justification. Therefore being justified by faith,*
> *we have peace with God through our Lord Jesus*
> *Christ:* (Romans 4:24-5:1).

This is the awesome, magnificent, glorious, merciful Heavenly Father God who created us and designed our roles. He always provides for His creation in a way that is far superior to anything we could possibly imagine. He turned the curse of death into a blessing through Jesus Christ. In the same manner, He will turn the "curse" of a woman's desire to control the man, into a blessing for all women who will trust in Him.

The Second Benefit

The second benefit that God included within the penalty for the woman's sin concerns her need for protection from deception. Women were created by God to be responders, companions, and helpmates to their own husbands. These characteristics make women excellent helpers to anyone in leadership. Therein lies the danger. Because women are characteristically helpers, they are susceptible to responding to the allurements of evil deception, as occurred in Genesis 3:1-5. It was not only the first woman who fell for persuasive lies; God says that all women are vulnerable to deception.

> *But I suffer not a woman to teach, nor to usurp*
> *authority over the man, but to be in silence. For*
> *Adam was first formed, then Eve. And Adam*
> *was not deceived, but the woman being deceived*
> *was in the transgression* (1 Timothy 2:12-14).

Deceived women are easily defrauded, beguiled, cheated, and mislead. Through the centuries deceivers have misled women by appealing to their desire for autonomy, or to their lust for knowledge. Such beguiled women are then easily used to tempt their men to oppose God's will, just as Eve was used by Satan to tempt Adam. Because women are easily deceived, they need protection from those who would take advantage of this weakness. Therefore, God offers women protection by giving them leadership – through their husbands. In this manner, God has turned the cursing of subjection into the blessing of protection for those women who trust God and defer to their husband's leadership.

But, Men Are Sinners, Too!

It may be difficult at this point to understand how being subject to a man's authority can actually be beneficial to a woman. After all, the man sinned knowingly and deliberately, while the woman was simply misled. Any woman knows that men are subject to error, as well as to deliberate selfishness and sin. No man is always going to make good decisions, even with the best of intentions.

Therefore, a woman's first reaction to the command to submit to her husband's rule is often fear, anger, or even shock that God could possibly mean **that**! Her "desire" to control her husband and the realization that her earthly life, both present and future, is dependent on the decisions of another person frightens her. All kinds of "but what ifs?" come to her mind. She can foresee that submitting to another's rule leaves her vulnerable, not only to error, but to intentional maltreatment as well. It is quite natural for a woman to fear that her man might take unfair advantage of his position of authority over her. It is also natural for her to attempt to maintain control over any decision that affects her. So then, how does a woman ever dare to trust in any man's leadership? She is able, because the Biblical woman's protection is **not** dependent solely on the character of her husband. It is the character of God that provides security. When a woman submits to her husband, she is actually living out her trust in God.

> *For after this manner in the old time the holy*
> *women also,* **who trusted in God**, *adorned*
> *themselves, being in subjection unto their own*
> *husbands:* (1 Peter 3:5). (Emphasis added.)

It is conceivable that a modern daughter of Eve may reject the idea that she needs protection from deception, even though God says that she does. But her disbelief does nothing to alter God's truth. Neither does her rejection alter God's judgment on her disobedience. Any woman, who rejects God's provision for her protection and His gift of her husband's rule over her desire to control, constructs a barrier between herself and the blessings within His plan. A woman who insists on being outside her husband's leadership places herself outside God's protection. In this vulnerable position, she is subject to the harmful effects of her own inherent weaknesses. Consequently, she is susceptible, not only to the deceitfulness of Satan, but also to the convincing arguments of all those who would seduce her away from the truth about her womanhood. In addition, she is totally subject to the self-delusion that is created by her own pride and lust. When she persists in living outside God's plan, cursing remains cursing and cannot be overcome – even with all her human abilities.

The realization of the blessings and benefits incorporated within God's judgment on the sin of the woman is achieved only when a woman replaces her own desire for personal autonomy with a complete trust in God. When a woman obeys God by allowing her husband to lead, God Himself will stand as an impenetrable protective shield and defend her from outside deception. In this protected position, cursing is overcome and turned to blessing.

In the next chapter we will look at the principles of authority that God has instituted for the benefit of His creation. I confess

I cannot think of enough adjectives to describe the awesomeness of our God and the intricacies of His system of authority. His design for sinful men and women to be able to live in harmony is so magnificent that it defies human words to explain. Nevertheless, I pray that He will use my inadequate words to awaken many Christian women not only to understand His provision, but also to rejoice in actually living within His design.

CHAPTER V

PRINCIPLES OF AUTHORITY

Authority! Here is a word that is bitterly despised by all rebels. An attitude of distrust and disrespect toward anyone in a position of leadership is prevalent today even among normally law-abiding people. Negative attitudes toward the concept of authority originate from man's misunderstandings about the proper meaning of, purpose for, and application of authority. These misunderstandings, added to personal experiences with dictators who have misused their power, have caused many people to fear and reject the concept of authority completely. Nevertheless, we need to understand the principles of authority so that we will not be deceived into a programmed response against the very system God has established for our freedom.

Why do so many people dislike the principle of authority? One reason is that where there are positions of authority, logic dictates that there are also subordinate positions to those authorities. The concept of subjection is even more antagonistic to the human will than is the concept of authority – and therein lies most women's true objection. It is much easier to accept one's own responsibility *as* the authority (such as a parent over children) than it is to accept personal subjection *to* an authority (such as a wife in submission to her husband).

Although this chapter is not actually about submission, it must be pointed out that objections to the concept of authority often stem from our own desire for autonomy. If you are feeling a little hesitant at this point, you are not unusual. Most of us feel at least a twinge of apprehension when confronted with this important subject. (Let me put your mind at ease, there is a difference between submission and blind obedience. We will learn about this vital difference in the next chapter.) For now, keep in mind that Eve wanted to be in control of her life, and you are a descendent of Eve and heir to her curse. While you read this chapter, try to set aside any objections to the concept of authority that have been caused by those people who have misused their power. Instead, allow God to reveal how His system was designed to bless and protect you. Do not let Satan deceive you, as he deceived Eve, into rejecting the peace and security God has ordained for your benefit. Resentment of authority will only close your mind to God's will for your life.

First, we will look at a generalized definition of authority. From that definition we will study some characteristics of God's supreme authority and then determine which principles apply to our subject – womanhood.

The General Definition of Authority

The definition of authority is: "the right to rule; the power to act, decide, command, and judge." [3] It is the right to set policy, the rulership position necessary to command subordinates, and the power to administer judgment to those who disobey and to reward those who conform.

At first glance, it might appear that authority is unbridled power that could easily be used to oppress those who are its subjects. Although it is true that there are, and always have been, those who abuse the power of authority, these exceptions do not alter the principle. The abuse of authority perpetrated by man only proves that mankind is sinful and that Satan's influence continues to exists in the world. Nevertheless, under God the power of authority is not without controls or limits. God has established rules and boundaries to govern the use of all authority. Even more importantly, God is always in control. He has the position and the ability to enforce His will over all other authorities.

God is the Ultimate Authority

For the LORD most high is terrible; he is a great King over all the earth (Psalm 47:2).

That men may know that thou, whose name alone is JEHOVAH, art the most high over all the earth (Psalm 83:18).

The word translated *Most High* is a title, and is only used in Scripture for God. [4] This title is never conferred upon a member of the human race. It is a title used only to describe God's position of absolute authority. He is the *Most High;* there is none other above Him with any right to rule.

I blessed the most High, and I praised and honoured him that liveth for ever, whose dominion is an everlasting dominion, and his kingdom is from generation to generation: (Daniel 4:34).

This passage recognizes the infinite extent of God's rule. There is no end to the reign of God. His timelessness strikes a sobering contrast to the insignificant period of time in which a human authority can exercise rulership. God is always in control!

But our God is in the heavens: he hath done whatsoever he hath pleased (Psalm 115:3).

> *...Shall the thing formed say to him that formed it, Why hast thou made me thus? Hath not the potter power over the clay, of the same lump to make one vessel unto honour, and another unto dishonour?* (Romans 9:20b-21).

God is the Creator. He has the right to rule whatever He creates. In other words, He has the total right to rule His creatures according to His will.

> *And all the inhabitants of the earth are reputed as nothing: and he doeth according to his will in the army of heaven, and among the inhabitants of the earth: and none can stay his hand, or say unto him, What doest thou?*
> (Daniel 4:35).

"And all the inhabitants of the earth are reputed as nothing" is a relative statement. It establishes a relationship between God's position of absolute authority (right to rule) and mankind's position of authority. Nebuchadnezzer, the speaker in this verse, is king over a mighty kingdom, and he is saying that even as king he has no right to say to God, "What are you doing?"

The conclusion that we can draw from these verses and from many others on the subject is that God, as our Creator, has the right to set the policy for all His creation according to His own will. He has the ultimate position of rulership above all the creatures whereby He may direct their actions. He also has the power to administer justice; in other words, He has the power to punish evil and to praise good. Since ultimate authority belongs to God, He is entitled to delegate any legitimate right to rule.

No Authority Exists Except As Appointed by God

> *Let every soul be subject unto the higher powers. For there is no power but of God: the powers that be are ordained of God* (Romans 13:1).

The Greek word translated "power" means "authority, the right to decide or act, ruling or official powers." [5] God commands *every* individual to place himself willingly under the positions of human rulership, which exists above him. How do we dare to do this? We can submit to our authorities because, as *Romans 13:1* states, no ruling power exists except through God. Every position of human authority that He has established remains under His control. The word translated "ordained" means "to place, station, appoint or determine someone into an official position over others." [6] It is the Greek word from which the theological term "institution" is derived. The three basic institutions defined in Scripture, which affects all humans, are government, marriage, and family. God has instituted all existing positions of rulership that govern His creatures, God's purpose for all rulers is to carry out His will and to administer justice to those under His rule.

God's Word gives specific boundaries to each institution's power and defines limits for the extent of its authority. These boundaries include defining those who are subject to each authority, as well as the extent to which those subjects must submit. For example, while parents have the right to rule their children, they do not have the right to make their children steal.

What About Evil Rulers?

Any problems arising from the abuse of human authority are not the fault of God's principles, but are due to mankind's failure to function properly according to God's Word. God could at any time remove from his position of authority any individual who oversteps his boundaries, but He often allows such a one to remain in his position of power in order to discipline, or to strengthen the character of, those who are suffering under unfair leadership. The pressure that God allows to come into our lives is intended to develop our trust in God, our dependence on His Word, and to strengthen our relationship with Him. God allows us to be under the exact kind of rulership that will fulfill His plan for each of us.

The life of Joseph is an example of how God works in the life of a believer in spite of an evil ruler (See Genesis 39-50). His brothers sold Joseph into slavery to an ungodly ruler who had the power to do whatever he willed with his slave. In fact, Joseph was unjustly accused and thrown into prison. God used these evil people and seemingly unfair situations to draw Joseph closer to Him. Subsequently, Joseph glorified God through the interpretation of his fellow prisoner's dreams and eventually the interpretation of Pharaoh's dreams. The pressure that Joseph withstood was rewarded – he was promoted to the second-in-command of the government, his family was saved from famine, and Israel was blessed through his faithfulness. Joseph later acknowledged God's ability to work in spite of the evil intentions of others, when he said to his brothers: *But as for you, ye thought evil against me; but God meant it unto good, to bring to pass, as it is this day, to save many people alive* (Genesis 50:20). Joseph's submission to his rightful authority under the worst of conditions is a testimony to any woman in a difficult marriage.

The Authority Structure for the Institution of Marriage

One of the most important authority structures for a Christian woman is the institution of marriage. Since this structure governs a major portion of a woman's life, it is vital that she fully comprehends God's plan for its function.

> *But I would have you know, that the head of every man is Christ; and the head of the woman is the man; and the head of Christ is God*
> (1 Corinthians 11:3).

This verse clearly establishes God's ordained authority structure for marriage. It reveals that the husband is the head of the family and that wives do not have equal authority in marriage. The Christian husband's authority is not without limits, however, since Christ is the ultimate head (authority) over the man. This verse also reveals that even Christ is under authority: the authority of God the Father.

It is important for a wife to understand thoroughly what God has to say about her husband's position of leadership. Otherwise, her tendency will be to overtly resist, or to quietly resent, her husband's position of authority. Every Christian wife answers directly to God for obeying His Word regarding submission to her husband's authority. This means that she must know the areas of her own accountability as a helpmate, and she must also know the areas in which her husband alone is accountable.

God's Word states in Genesis 3:16, and 1 Corinthians 11:3; Ephesians 5:23-24; 1 Timothy 3:2-5 and 3:12 that the husband, not the wife, is accountable to God for the rule of the home. The husband's leadership position is an obligatory responsibility. This responsibility does not leave him free to do as he pleases; he is accountable to God for performing his leadership duties according to God's instructions. Although a wife does not have equal earthly authority with her husband, she is still personally accountable to perform her helpmate duties in accordance with God's instructions.

The authority structure of marriage should not be seen as a denouncement meant to shame women, to oppress them, or to demean their value. God did not give the husband the position of leadership because the man possessed more merit or status than the woman. Both men and women have equal status and merit before God. For instance, the Biblical instructions for obtaining and maintaining a personal relationship with God are the same for both men and women. God provides each man and woman protection from eternal condemnation through their personal acceptance of Jesus Christ as his or her Savior. Similarly, every man and woman is equally accountable to God for obedience to His Word, which includes abiding by His authority structure in marriage.

An Earthly Marriage, a Spiritual Picture

*For the husband is the head of the wife, even as
Christ is the head of the church: and he is the
saviour of the body. Therefore as the church is
subject unto Christ, so let the wives be to their
own husbands in every thing* (Ephesians 5:23-24).

The husband's position of authority is necessary for the proper and orderly function of family government. However, this structure has a far greater purpose than just the establishment of a peaceful household. Christian marriage is designed to portray to the world an image of the bond between believers and Christ. The roles in marriage are pictures of the spiritual authority of Christ (the husband) over believers (the wife) and of the believers' submissive bond and oneness with Christ. Presenting a Christ-like image in marriage should be the goal of every Christian couple. Yet, many marriages today do not operate according to God's ordained authority structure. This is one reason that Christians are losing their impact on today's society. A marriage that does not operate within God's design presents to the world a distorted view of the authority of Christ over believers and their submission to Him.

The man's headship over his family is of such importance to God that a man desiring to hold an office in the church is Biblically disqualified if he has been lax in his leadership responsibilities at home (1 Timothy 3:2-5 and 3:12). The proven ability of a man to lead his wife and train his children is a prerequisite to his auditioning for a position of leadership over a portion of God's flock. Whether a husband becomes a leader in the church or not, it remains true that he must be the head of his family, generating the submission of his wife, in order to properly represent to the world Christ's headship of the church and the church's submission to Christ.

The Biblical wife is privileged to play a role in the inter-linking spiritual significance of her helpmate position and Christ's submission to God the Father. When a wife grasps the spiritual implications of her helpmate role it takes on a greater significance. While armies of Eve's rebellious daughters are being deceived into repeating Satan's call for the overthrow of God's authority, she is not swayed. A Biblical wife submits to her husband because she desires to live according to God's will – not because her husband is a perfect leader. She knows that no matter what happens, God is in control. Therefore, if God allows pressure into her life because of a husband who does not lead well, she seeks His purpose and freely submits to His will. She should not try to find ways to escape from that which God has allowed into her life.

> *And we know that all things work together for good to them that love God, to them who are the called according to his purpose*
> (Romans 8:28).

> *What shall we then say to these things? If God be for us, who can be against us?*
> (Romans 8:31).

Now that we understand God's system of authority in marriage, we are prepared to study the concept of submission to authority. The next chapter will cover the critical difference between submission and obedience. It is my prayer that the reader will find this information both exciting and liberating.

CHAPTER VI

SUBMISSION IS NOT THE SAME AS OBEDIENCE

Biblical submission is **not** synonymous with obedience. Nevertheless, even Christian women frequently define submission as oppression, slavery, or even blind obedience. This chapter will attempt to dispel such misconceptions about Biblical submission and reveal its spiritual significance within the husband and wife relationship. In order to understand the critical difference between submission and obedience, we first need to discover the Biblical definition of each word.

Obedience

God's Word uses two distinctive Greek words, one for obedience and the other for submission, when referring to the function of various subordinates within governing establishments. The Greek word *Hupakouo* is normally used in Scripture for obedience. Its literal meaning is "under the hearing of commands." A Biblical command for obedience is often followed by a promise of blessing to the subject who complies, or with a warning of negative consequences to the person who rebels. Under the command for obedience, the subject is offered no alternative but to obey, without debate or question. The appointed authority enforces compliance, executes judgment, and stands responsible for the results of his rule. The responsibility of the subject under obedience is to do what he is told. [7]

An example of the concept of obedience is found in Colossians 3:22: *Servants, obey in all things your masters according to the flesh; not with eyeservice, as menpleasers; but in singleness of heart, fearing God.*

Christian slaves were instructed to remain obedient to their masters and to serve wholeheartedly, as if they were serving the Lord Himself (Colossians 3:23-25). The following verses give us two more examples of God's use of the word "obedience." In the first passage God commands children to obey their parents.

> *Children, obey your parents in the Lord: for this is right. Honour thy father and mother; (which is the first commandment with promise;) That it may be well with thee, and thou mayest live long on the earth* (Ephesians 6:1-3).

The second passage concerns the importance of obedience to God.

> *And to you who are troubled rest with us, when the Lord Jesus shall be revealed from heaven with his mighty angels, In flaming fire taking vengeance on them that know not God, and that* **obey not** *the gospel of our Lord Jesus Christ: Who shall be punished with everlasting destruction from the presence of the Lord, and from the glory of his power;*
> (2 Thessalonians 1:7-9). (Emphasis added.)

Obedience to the gospel of Jesus Christ refers to the personal acceptance of Christ as the only way to receive eternal salvation (Acts 4:12). This example warns that the consequences for this disobedience (rejection of Christ as Savior) will be everlasting separation from the presence and power of the Lord.

Submission

The second Greek word used in the Bible when referring to the function of subordinates is *Hupotasso*, normally used in Scripture for submission. Literally, submission means "under placement or position, status or rank." This word is used by the writers of Scripture to refer to the positions and attitudes of subjects under the authority of their government (1 Peter 2:13-15), to believers under the teaching authority of their pastors (Hebrews 13:17b *"... submit to them for they watch for your souls... "*), and of wives under the leadership of their husbands (Colossians 3:18). The Biblical definition of submission includes the willing and positive response of a subordinate to his rightful authority. The submissive subject **consciously and freely yields** his or her own will to the will of God or to their God-ordained human authority. [8]

An example of Biblical submission is Christ's surrender to God the Father in the Garden of Gethsemane just prior to His crucifixion. Christ's example reveals that submission is not an act of unthinking obedience, but instead, it is a conscious act of choosing to yield one's will to the will of his authority.

> *And he was withdrawn from them about a stone's cast, and kneeled down, and prayed, Saying, Father, if thou be willing, remove this cup from me: nevertheless not my will, but thine, be done* (Luke 22:41-42).

The Difference Between Submission and Obedience

When God commands a person to obey, his or her duty is to comply. For example, a child is unquestionably to obey the authority of his parents; and the parents are instructed to enforce compliance, even against the child's will when necessary. However, when God commands a wife to submit to her husband's authority, He is requiring more of her than mere compliance. He is calling her to choose to submit just as Jesus Christ submitted to God the Father's authority.

In **Chapter V, "Principles of Authority,"** we saw that while a wife's submission to the authority of her husband is necessary for a peaceful family life, the spiritual significance is greater. Christ's relationship with God the Father and the Church's relationship with Christ are models for the relationship between husband and wife in marriage.

> *For the husband is the head of the wife, even as Christ is the head of the church: and he is the saviour of the body. Therefore as the church is subject unto Christ, so let the wives be to their own husbands in every thing* (Ephesians 5:23-24).

1 Peter 3 complements the spiritual picture of Ephesians 5:23-24 by revealing the Christ-like manner in which a wife is to submit to her husband.

> *Likewise, ye wives, be in subjection to your own husbands; that, if any obey not the word, they also may without the word be won by the conversation of the wives;* (1 Peter 3:1).

While some women chafe at submission and look for exceptions to the rule, the Biblical woman will ask, "In what same manner does God want me to submit?"

"Likewise, ye wives, be in subjection…" is explained previously in 1 Peter 2:21-23:

For even hereunto were ye called: because Christ also suffered for us, leaving us an example, that ye should follow his steps: Who did no sin, neither was guile found in his mouth: Who, when he was reviled, reviled not again; when he suffered, he threatened not; but committed himself to him that judgeth righteously: (1 Peter 2:21-23).

These verses reveal that the word, "Likewise" in 1 Peter 3:1 refers to the way Christ submitted to the plan of God. Our sinless Christ had both the power and the right to escape the injustice of being punished for sin He did not commit. However, He submitted to the worst of injustices so that He might fulfill the plan of God. He provided a pathway to eternal salvation by means of His submission. The "Likewise" in 1 Peter 3:1 reveals that:

1. A Biblical wife should also commit herself to "Him that judges righteously."

2. She submits even to a husband who is not under the Word so she will not become a barrier between him and God.

3. "In the same manner" as Christ, a Biblical wife is to maintain an attitude of willing submission.

4. Through Christ as her perfect example a wife can submit to God because she trusts Him implicitly, just as Christ trusted Him.

5. With the knowledge of God's plan for her life and her shield of faith (belief) in God, she can willingly submit to her husband's leadership.

As you can see, the phrase "in the same manner" lifts the concept of a wife's submission to her husband above its earthly purpose of a peaceful family life. "In the same manner" highlights the importance of every believer's conscious choice to willingly submit to the will of God.

The Submissive Wife's Accountability to God

Another major difference between submission and obedience can be found in the level of responsibility that God places on a subordinate for his or her own actions and attitudes. Acts 5:29 tells us that obedience to God takes precedence, if there is a conflict between God's command and man's decree. A Biblically submissive wife is willing to comply, but, realizing that she still remains accountable to God for personal sin, she may choose to disobey if her husband's request or command is a known violation of one of God's direct commands. If noncompliance is necessary, however, the Biblically submissive wife continues to maintain the proper attitude of respect for her husband's leadership position and for his overall right to lead. This action might be called, "submissive noncompliance."

Submissive Noncompliance

A Biblical example of submissive noncompliance is found in the sixth chapter of *Daniel*. In this passage the king made a law "...*whosoever shall ask a petition of any god or man for thirty days, except of thee, O king, shall be cast into the den of lions"* (Daniel 6:7b).

Obedience to the king's decree would have caused Daniel to sin against a direct command of God: *"Thou shalt have no other gods before me"* (Exodus 20:3). Therefore, it was necessary for Daniel to disobey the king's law. However, was his disobedience an act of self-righteous rebellion, or was it submissive noncompliance? It is imperative that we examine Daniel's attitude toward his king for the answer to this question.

First of all, Daniel maintained a close personal relationship with God, even though it meant that he had to disobey the king.

> *Now when Daniel knew that the writing was*
> *signed, he went into his house; and his windows*
> *being open in his chamber toward Jerusalem,*
> *he kneeled upon his knees three times a day, and*
> *prayed, and gave thanks before his God, as he*
> *did aforetime* (Daniel 6:10).

Secondly, there is no indication that Daniel had a rebellious or defensive attitude toward his role as a subject under a king. He previously submitted to the king's authority in all things, and he did not disobey until the king passed a new law that directly opposed God's expressed will: that believers worship Him alone, praying, and giving thanks. Although Daniel knew the dire consequences of choosing to disobey in this instance, he did not do so defiantly, nor did he run away from those consequences. Daniel continued to recognize the king's right as a duly appointed authority to execute punishment.

> *Then the king commanded, and they brought*
> *Daniel, and cast him into the den of lions*
> (Daniel 6:16a).

Thirdly, Daniel remained respectful of his king's position of authority. He was free from any rebellious or self-righteous attitudes before, during, and after his disobedience. Daniel's speech after God delivered him from the lions is a perfect example of willing submission to an authority in a situation requiring submissive noncompliance.

> *Then said Daniel unto the king, O king, live*
> *forever. My God hath sent his angel, and hath*
> *shut the lions' mouths, that they have not hurt*
> *me: forasmuch as before him innocency was*
> *found in me; and also before thee, O king, have*
> *I done no hurt* (Daniel 6:21-22).

Notice that Daniel said, "O king, live forever," to an authority that had just ordered his death.

Daniel's example of submission is a far cry from the defiant "I will never allow a man tell me what to do," that we hear many women say today. Such outcries usually come from women who try to justify their refusal to obey God's command by claiming that their husband's *might* ask them to do something that would violate their personal rights. Such women lie in wait, expecting their husbands to err, so that their before-the-fact attitude of non-submission will be vindicated. They often fabricate "what ifs" and treat the rare misuses of their husbands' authority as if they were common, everyday events. (I believe the percentage of husbands who actually ask their **godly** wives to sin is very, very small. Therefore, for most women this is a moot point, born more from a desire to escape submission entirely, rather than a true concern over wronging God.) The attitude of women who attempt to pre-justify non-submission is a continuation of the garden-variety rebelliousness that has existed since the fall of mankind. By contrast, Daniel's example is a testimony of what is possible when a believer obeys God by submitting to human authorities that actually are unrighteous in their actions.

No, obedience and submission are not synonymous. The difference, however, is not necessarily seen in one's overt actions. Often, true submission can only be seen by the respectful attitude a woman has toward her authority – before, during, and after any directive. For instance, Sarah overtly obeyed Abraham: *"Even as Sara obeyed Abraham, calling him lord: whose daughters ye are, as long as ye do well, and are not afraid with any amazement"* (1 Peter 3:6). This Scripture passage reveals to us that this noble woman's actions were more than mere obedience because she called Abraham *lord*. Her "obedience" was the act, but she also possessed an attitude of submission. Sarah, like other holy women, was able to submit to her husband respectfully because she trusted God: *"For after this manner in the old time the holy women also, who trusted in God, adorned themselves, being in subjection unto their own husbands:"* (1 Peter 3:5).

When you trust God, as did Sarah, while you submit to your husband, you join a very old and revered family. You too are a noble woman, a spiritual daughter of Sarah, when your absolute trust in the integrity of God supersedes your claim to personal rights. As a spiritual daughter you are also a sister of many holy women throughout history who chose true submission over begrudged obedience.

In Conclusion

Obedience is an external act of compliance, while submission toward any authority is a respectful attitude that comes before, during, and after **all** actions. Where a list of rules and commands must precede obedience, submission precedes rules and supersedes law. True submission is the willingness to follow **even before** all of the details are known. Submission includes a woman's freedom of choice – her choice to obey God by freely yielding herself to the authority He has ordained in her life. Her willingness to comply involves trust – her absolute trust in the integrity of the God who designed her role and included submission to authority within His plan. Submission is the natural result of a Biblical woman's abiding trust in God, and it is the fruit of her desire to do His will.

It is my prayer that this chapter has encouraged you to commit yourself to the One who *"judgeth righteously"* and to His design for womanhood. May you experience the freedom that comes from living your life by the Word of God.

CHAPTER VII

WHY ARE MEN SO DIFFERENT?

Most women think that men are strange and difficult to understand. Why are little boys so physically active, noisy, and aggressive? Why do they like dirt and hate cleanliness? Why are men more comfortable being in the driver's seat of the car or controlling the remote? Why are so many of them interested in everything motorized? Why do they enjoy action, power, and anything that goes VAROOM?

If we compare scientific studies on the psychological and emotional make-up of the male and female, it becomes evident that there are many areas of dissimilarity. By the age of ten or eleven girls have greater verbal ability than boys, while boys excel in visual-spatial ability. It can also be observed that young boys are more aggressive both physically and verbally than girls. Male aggression usually emerges as early as social play begins, around two years of age. Boys appear to be especially stimulated to bursts of high activity and competition by the presence of other boys.

We know that men's voices are a different pitch than women's, their bodies are shaped differently, and some deodorant ads say they even perspire differently. Also, most women think that men possess vastly overdeveloped egos. On top of everything else women have a difficult time understanding the man's bizarre way of thinking. Why did God create the male sex to be so different from the female sex?

Let us begin with the principle that God's original creation of mankind was designed with intent and for a valuable purpose. This means that all emotional, psychological, and physical differences between men and women were created as an integral part of God's plan for mankind. He created each sex with unique bodies, distinctive thinking patterns, and specific characteristics. Such thinking patterns and characteristics are not taught; instead, they are a part of the inner being of each sex. [9] However as we can observe there exists a problem with how men and women often exercise their individual unique traits. Why?

The characteristics of mankind were originally created in God's own image (Genesis 1:27). Therefore, before the fall, mankind's unique attributes would have been perfectly implemented into every day life. But, ever since sin entered into the world people have been born in the likeness of Adam: *And Adam lived an hundred and thirty years, and begat a son in his own likeness, after his image*; (Genesis 5:3) – that is with the nature of sinfulness. The created traits of both men and women are now tainted by sin. As a child grows, internal pressures (the nature of sin) and external factors (poor parental training) can seriously distort inborn traits. Two examples are: a little girl being trained to fulfill the masculine role, and a little boy being trained to be effeminate. Nevertheless, the unique characteristics of each sex were originally meant to facilitate the fulfillment of God's design for men and women. With understanding of the original purpose for each sex's uniqueness and the power of God in the lives of believers, those purposes can again be fulfilled.

Women Were Created to Be Responders

Evidence of a woman's responsive nature exists within the emotional patterns that comprise the "mothering instinct." Women are also endowed with a depth of appreciation, sensitivity, and compassion for others. They tend to be more affectionate and to possess a greater desire to please others than do men. These and other basically feminine attributes stem from the emotionally responsive nature of the woman's soul. This natural responsiveness and its manifestations are essential for women to function as Biblical helpmates and as mothers.

Men Were Created to Be Initiators

The distinct characteristic of the man's soul is the drive to initiate leadership. The man is also physically stronger, more aggressive, competitive, and very possessive – ideal traits for protecting and providing for his wife and family. Even the strange way men think becomes not so strange after all, but even comprehensible, when we recognize God's original purpose for men. As we will see, this purpose also helps explain the reason for the male ego.

Ego

A dictionary definition of ego is: "The 'I' or self of any person; a person as thinking, feeling and willing, and distinguishing itself from the selves of others and from objects of its thought." Ego is also defined as self-esteem or self-image. [10] Ego can be positively expressed or negatively expressed, but its purest definition is simply recognition of self as distinct from others.

The way men view themselves (their egos) and how they relate to others reveal general masculine tendencies. Men are assertive and competitive amongst themselves, they have a strong desire to succeed, and they automatically desire to lead others – especially women. At an early age boys often feel protective toward their mothers and sisters, and they will respond quite seriously to the idea of being the "man of the house" while Daddy is away. Even in very young boys the idea of leading and protecting their women corresponds to their masculine egos and makes them feel valuable, needed, and good about themselves. These are just a few traits that appear to be expressions of the male ego. A man with a healthy male ego is aware of, and is comfortable with, his manliness.

A Definition for Manliness

Manliness is the expression of a healthy male ego and is an important component in the way a man views himself. It is the part of a man that gives him the confidence, courage, objectivity, and initiative to be a leader. Proper manliness initiates a desire to protect and provide, which are two of the ways a well-balanced man expresses his love for his wife and children. The male ego and masculinity are so closely intertwined that if you destroy a man's ego, you will also destroy his manliness.

Egotism

The sin nature distorts the legitimate ego as it does every other human trait. For instance, it can distort the human ability to love and can cause true love for the benefit of another to be altered into a grasping and egocentric love of self. Likewise, sin can distort the ego, and cause an individual (both male and female) to have an inflated and inappropriate ego.

A man who has an inappropriate ego will manifest either aggressive egotism or passive egotism. Some of the manifestations of aggressive egotism are exaggerated self-importance, sinful pride, cruelty, and a domineering attitude towards those under his leadership. A few of the manifestations of a man's passive egotism are sinful pride, insecurity, cowardliness, and a refusal to lead his wife and family.

Anyone who has watched young boys at play has observed untrained egos. Most boys begin very early in life wanting to be the person in charge and willing to do almost anything to top one another. They compete in everything, including which one is the biggest, and which one can talk first or loudest. Each boy's confidence is undaunted; he is positive he will be the one to win the game (by defeating others), or that his dad can whip everyone else's dad. The innate inner drive to excel is a good and natural part of a boy's maleness, but the tactics for achieving this desire are distorted by his untrained and unrestrained nature to sin, resulting in immature egotism.

It is God's design for parents to restrain their sons' sin natures without destroying their created characteristics. Parents are to train their sons to express the inner drive to excel, but in acceptable ways. However, because of the lack of proper child training of boys for quite a few years, we now have a large number of adult men with distorted egos. As a result, many men today exhibit self-centered, overbearing egotism, or what some may call "macho." There also appears to be an even greater number of male egos that have been damaged severely enough to produce insecurity, indecisiveness, and passivity. Passive male egos are typically the result of a male's response to domineering mothers or ridiculing fathers, and then compounded by domineering wives. The chart at the end of the chapter will help you picture in your mind the difference between a healthy male ego and the distortions of a man's ego.

Compounded Problems

If it is true that a large percentage of today's adult men possess damaged male egos in one form or the other, then it follows that most wives have inherited one of these problems. However, a wife who has a negative attitude toward even the proper male ego compounds any legitimate problem that might already exist. For example, when a normally passive husband attempts to assert himself, his wife will compound his passivity if she constantly finds fault with his efforts. In ignorance this wife discourages her husband's attempted leadership (a portion of his legitimate male ego) and pushes him farther from his manly role. Unwittingly, she encourages the destruction of whatever remains of her husband's masculinity and his natural inclination to lead. This husband will eventually quit trying to lead and abdicate his leadership role entirely to his wife. A wife's negative attitudes toward the expressions of her husband's ego are counterproductive to the role of a supportive helpmate and tend to compound any existing problems.

Samson and Delilah Allegory

The well-known Bible account of Samson and Delilah reveals much truth about the fragile nature of a man's manliness. For the sake of our discussion, we will consider Samson's hair to be analogous to the strength of his legitimate ego (his manhood). Delilah is analogous to any woman's ability to destroy her Samson's manhood.

A man's ego is extremely vulnerable and sensitive to attacks by the Delilahs in his life (mother, girl friends, wife). When a "Delilah" derides or rejects her Samson's expressions of manhood, she heaps upon him feelings of discouragement and weakness. Attacks can come in the form of a general attitude of rejection or by sharp cutting words of belittlement. "I don't trust you." "You are so stupid and clumsy." "Why can't you be more like Fred?" "Your competitiveness with Jim is just silly and egotistical." "You havn't got a clue what a real man is." These are just a few put-downs that cut straight through the heart of any man's ego.

Cutting off the real Samson's hair rendered him physically weak and ineffective. In a similar sense a wife's rejection of her husband's male ego results in the weakening of his manliness. When a man's legitimate male ego is weakened by rejection or ridicule, he will not have the strength, courage, or confidence to provide effective leadership. Consequently, his weakened ability to lead will limit his desire to protect and provide for his wife. It even limits his manly expression of love. The results can be devastating. Many marriages have been destroyed by a husband having his ego flattered by another woman, *after first* having it flattened by his wife.

Attacks on your own Samson's manliness can be either an overt and vocal refusal to accept his leadership, or it can be subtler. There are many effective ways to give your husband subtle "rejection notices." You can ignore what he tells you about anything. Treat his attempts to lead as unwelcome interferences in your life. Politely listen to him, disregard his wishes, and then do whatever you want to do. Be certain he understands that, on your list of priorities, his needs come after your own. Go your own way, and "do your own thing." These are just some of the ways you can effectively cut off your husband's "hair" and render his manhood weak and powerless.

Men who submit for a sufficient period of time to having their "hair cut off" usually become the exact opposite of what God intended. Their manly leadership drives give way to passivity, default of responsibility, fear of failure, and indecisiveness. The drive to protect women is designed to produce bravery, but when thwarted consistently, it gives way to cowardliness. When their manly drive to provide is long denied, it becomes difficult for men to accept responsibility for their own support, let alone take responsibility for the support of others.

On the other hand, a husband who has his wife's support and appreciation is encouraged to develop the more desirable traits inherent within the healthy male ego. For instance, appreciation for a man's drive to protect women encourages him toward selflessness and bravery. When a man's drive to provide for his family is encouraged, he develops a strong sense of responsibility toward others and a desire to achieve. A naturally passive man tends to become more assertive in his leadership and an aggressive man is more likely to consider the vulnerability of a submissive wife.

God made no mistake when He created the male ego. If a woman hopes to be a Biblical wife, she must have the compassionate, loving spirit of one who desires to accept her man as God has designed him. Understanding the necessity of the legitimate male ego with all its drives and functions is one of the first steps in becoming a supportive and encouraging helpmate. A wife can help repair her husband's bruised manhood (passive or aggressive), by simply being a Biblical wife. She can help by appreciating and encouraging her husband's God-given drives – even if he does not always express them perfectly.

Ego

Definition: That which recognizes self as distinct from others. The male ego should be developed into maturity for the man's role of leadership and conquering of the physical world

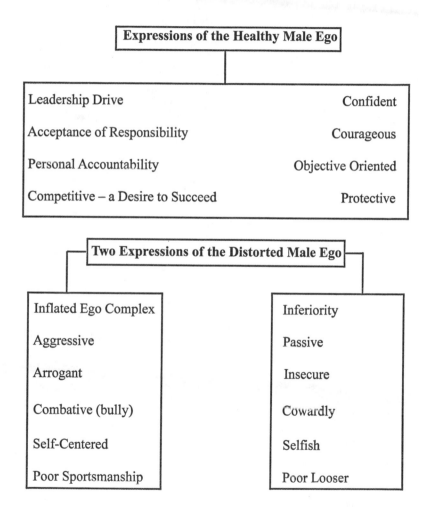

Expressions of the Healthy Male Ego

Leadership Drive

Acceptance of Responsibility

Personal Accountability

Competitive – a Desire to Succeed

Confident

Courageous

Objective Oriented

Protective

Two Expressions of the Distorted Male Ego

Inflated Ego Complex

Aggressive

Arrogant

Combative (bully)

Self-Centered

Poor Sportsmanship

Inferiority

Passive

Insecure

Cowardly

Selfish

Poor Looser

CHAPTER VIII

WHEN TWO HEADS ARE BETTER THAN ONE

Therefore shall a man leave his father and his mother, and shall cleave unto his wife: and they shall be one flesh (Genesis 2:24).

God's Word declares that marriage should merge two independent parts into one whole unit. It is not necessary for either part to lose its unique distinction in order to merge. In fact, the distinctions of the two is what makes "the one" possible. Marriage is like a jigsaw puzzle with its many unique pieces. Each piece has its own distinct shape and bears a portion of the whole picture. However, the manufacturer did not intend for the puzzle pieces to remain separated; instead, he intentionally designed them to fit perfectly together. While the puzzle pieces do not lose their distinct shapes when fitted together, it is only when the pieces become one that the whole picture emerges. In the same way, God intentionally designed the male and female, distinct in shape and function, to fit together perfectly in marriage. And like the puzzle pieces, both husband and wife retain individuality and uniqueness, while portraying a whole "picture" in the unity and oneness of marriage.

In order for a husband and wife to merge into one, it is extremely important for them to understand how their different ways of thinking combine to create oneness in their marriage.

Have you noticed times when you and your husband seem to be telling two different stories, even though you are describing the same event? Are you able to read "body language" and sense how people feel, while your husband thinks you are imagining things? Are you more interested in conveying the precise details, while details are less important to him (like the **exact** day he did such and such)? Have you ever tried to tell your husband something exciting, only to have him become impatient with your long narrative and say, "When are you going to get to the point?" Most women will say, "Yes, yes, yes, yes. Sometimes it is as if my husband and I live on two different planets." You do not live on two different planets, but you do think on two different planes. This chapter will help you see how both your husband's and your own unique thinking patterns are needed to make your marriage whole. (Honestly, your man's funny way of thinking was not created just to irritate you!)

A wife would usually accept that her husband is only half complete and needs her in order to be whole. However, she needs to realize that her attributes are only half of God's creation of mankind as well; she also needs her husband in order to be complete.

A Biblical helpmate complements her husband; she does not attempt to remodel his masculine thinking into feminine thinking or try to mold him into her own image. Too often in counseling situations and marriage seminars today a husband is exhorted to exchange his masculine thinking for his wife's feminine thinking. Sadly, this often results in modern men being trained to become their *wives* helpmates, rather than the other way around. It is true that men should understand and respect how a woman thinks, but it is not true or healthy for men to become feminized and abdicate their roles as men.

In a Biblical marriage, the wife benefits from the way her husband thinks, and he benefits from the way she thinks. Only a respectful blend of the two unique thinking patterns, as well as all the other unique qualities of both the husband and wife, will accomplish the oneness that God intends for marriage. God's intent in marriage is not accomplished when a man's qualities are obliterated and all that is left are feminine characteristics.

You might think that combining the different ways men and women think is like trying to mix oil and water. This is a natural conclusion, when we do not understand how such diverse thinking patterns can actually be compatible. When a man and woman live within God's design – the man as the head, the woman as his helpmate – their differences homogenize, and they are able to work together for a common purpose. Instead of operating as two separate and incomplete entities, they cooperate as one. Let us look at how these two types of thinking complement each other.

A Woman's Thinking

A woman's thinking normally includes how she feels about any topic. She is usually very observant of minute details and alert to the emotional reactions of others. A woman is typically quite verbal. This means that she thinks while she talks and talks while she thinks. She also tends to speak with an abundance of words. Because she is observant of details, effusive, and frequently led by her emotions, she rarely relates information in a "just-the-facts-ma'am" manner. No matter how intelligent she is, a woman's thinking is never far removed from her emotional reactions. Therefore, her presentation of data is usually dramatic, colorful, and descriptive.

A woman can have a very high IQ, but her pattern of thinking is inseparable from her femininity. She normally displays deeply intense emotions concerning the pleasure or pain of others. A woman's emotions create in her an affectionate, sensitive, and responsive nature. This sensitive nature causes her to be easily hurt when anyone, especially her father or her husband, is displeased with her.

Additionally, a woman has an inherent need for emotional, physical, and financial security. This is one reason that she appears to worry a lot. Admittedly, fathers and husbands who failed to provide this essential security have disillusioned many women in recent generations. Because of this sad fact, a woman who has been disappointed by men may try to harden herself against her inherent need for security. But, the emotional need for a man to take care of her, to love her and protect her, still cries out in her soul. Resident within a woman's soul is a powerful need for her man to provide for and protect her from harm. However, I am not suggesting that a man can, or even should, *ever* take the place of God in a woman's life. A husband is to be a complement and an earthly soul mate, but he cannot be expected to completely fill those deeper soul needs that only God can fill. Only He can heal damage that has been caused by people in the past. A woman can expect to find complete acceptance through her personal relationship with God. Her deepest need for absolute security and a completely satisfying relationship can only be found in God. Therefore, if you are one of those women who have been hurt by the men in your life, allow God to fulfill your need for security. He alone is your refuge.

> *In God is my salvation and my glory: the rock of my strength, and my refuge, is in God. Trust in him at all times; ye people, pour out your heart before him: God is a refuge for us. Selah* (Psalm 62:7-8).

Build this necessary relationship with God by learning His Word and leaning on His love and sovereign care. Do not use the hurts from your past as an excuse to disobey God's design for marriage. After all, while you are building your relationship with God and making Him first in your life, He just might work on and through your husband to give you a measure of earthly security as well. Even if your husband does not always fulfill His role, you can contentedly thrive on your personal relationship with God.

A Man's Thinking

A man tends to be less observant of the feelings of people and more attentive to issues. He is frequently less verbal than a woman and often meditates within himself rather than speaking while he thinks. A man tends to view things in a more facts-oriented manner. He is typically frank and uses short, to-the-point sentences when speaking. When a man must make a difficult decision, he usually does not include lengthy considerations about how people feel. He generally tries to set aside even his own feelings in order to maintain objective thinking. An exceptional leader will often refuse to dwell on the possible negative consequences of doing what is right before God because he does not want to be persuaded to act in self-protection. Maintaining objectivity and refusing to act in self-preservation, he can be more certain that his final decision is an unbiased one. His wife may mistakenly think that he does not care about the effect of his decisions, or that he is insensitive to the feelings of others. Additionally, she may believe that her husband is shutting her out of his thoughts because he meditates in silence. As a rule these assumptions are not true, but a wife may assume that they are, if she judges her husband's way of thinking by her own mental process and emotional responsiveness.

At first glance we might wonder how such diverse methods of thinking could ever be compatible. As we know, it is rare for either a man or a woman to understand the way the other thinks; each considers that his or her way is superior. Until men and women come to understand and appreciate the importance of and place for their different approaches to life, there will always be misunderstandings between them.

Putting Two Heads Together

As we saw in **Chapter VI**, God designed the different physical, emotional, and psychological make-up of each sex as a part of His plan. In their correct positions, and with their unique attributes exercised correctly, a man and woman are complimentary components in God's design of marriage. A woman's awareness of the feelings of others makes her more emotionally attentive as a helpmate, and her many feminine attributes prompt her towards selfless service to others. The man's objectivity makes him more adept in leadership, because his decisions are less likely to be influenced by emotions.

Let us look at an illustration that will reveal the differences in the thinking of men and women. Through this illustration we will see how both the emotional responsiveness of the woman and the more objective approach of the man are necessary in order to fulfill God's design in marriage.

Many toddlers cry when they are first put to bed, some even scream as if they are in great pain. They will also get out of bed repeatedly, call for their mommy, ask for a drink, or use any number of other resourceful tactics in order to remain awake.

A mother naturally responds emotionally when she believes her child is in need. This responsiveness motivates her to rush to her crying child, pick him up, comfort, and protect him. Even if she believes the child is not in pain, but simply trying to keep from going to sleep, it is difficult for her to deny comfort. She continues to worry that this time he may truly be in need. She may imagine that her child is afraid and allow him to sleep with her, she may conclude that he is hungry and over-feed him, or she may allow him to stay up until he falls over from exhaustion. It is easier for a woman to give needless comfort than it is for her to deny her child's demands. She may feel emotional stress even when she intellectually knows that it is better for the child if she does not give in to his desire to stay awake.

On the other hand, a man's normal response to a child's bedtime stay-up-as-long-as-possible ritual is usually without any emotional urgency to give comfort. The typical man will look for physical reasons for the distress, and if there are none readily apparent, he will usually recognize the child's strategy as an attempt to exercise control. Often a man can make a quick decision about how to stop such control techniques and he will follow through with little emotional response to the child's tears.

A man's objectivity in child training is a necessary balance to the woman's more emotional responsiveness. His suppression of emotional response enables him to more easily consider the long-range effects of his decisions and actions, while the woman is more concerned with easing the immediate distress. This does not mean that the man is without emotions; it simply means that his emotions are restrained in favor of more objective thinking.

The mother's feminine responsiveness enables her to tend to the physical and emotional needs of others. It prompts her toward loving and tender actions that are beneficial in child nurturing. Her sympathetic nature is perfect for giving comfort, but it must be mixed with objectivity when the child needs to learn the difficult lessons that are part of growing up. Emotional responsiveness alone can be undesirable for a child's overall welfare if it is not tempered by objectivity.

Conversely, the man's objectivity alone is not sufficient to meet all of a child's need all the time. When children are truly distressed, they need loving touches and comforting support for the proper development of their emotional security. Objectivity alone is cold comfort when a child truly needs sympathy or compassion. Feminine responsiveness and masculine objectivity must work *in unison* in order to provide a child with a balanced life. A child needs his mother's tender response to his present needs *and* he needs his father's objectivity in order to be properly trained for adult life.

I once had a conversation with a young father who put it this way: "My wife is concerned about making a healthy, happy child and she does a very good job. However, I am concerned with making a mature adult." This father recognized that his child needed his mother's nurturing, but he also realized that, as a father, his major concern was to train his son for adulthood. The mother was seeing the short-ranged needs, but the father had a longer-ranged mission.

It is important to realize that although a woman possesses many outstanding attributes, none of them are sufficient alone. A woman should never think that her special qualities are superior to a man's. Womanly characteristics are excellent when used as God intended, but they can also be exceedingly destructive when misapplied. Nurturing and protecting only, instead of objective child training will spoil a child. Catering to the whims of a child will create for him an unrealistic, me-centered world. He will continue as an adult to demand instant gratification; and this self-centeredness will motivate him to play on the emotions of others (especially women) in order to obtain his selfish desires.

The very attributes that make a woman warm and loving also create a susceptibility to rational blindness and emotional deception. A woman who is totally governed by her feelings is blinded to reality, and her intense emotional reactions can cause her to be easily manipulated by a clever decciver. Feminine qualities require balance. God gives the woman that balance through her husband's leadership. Her child will have a more balanced training for life if she does not allow her "feelings" to interfere with, or to negate, the effect of the father's more objective approach to child training.

Not only is balance needed in child training, but it is needed in all other areas of a woman's life as well. A wife's entire life will be more symmetrical when she trusts God's plan and submits to her husband's leadership. Another whole chapter could be written on how a woman's thinking helps to balance a man's thinking, but this book is not meant for men. However, even with this one-sided example, the point should be clear. When a man and a woman cooperatively "put their heads together," they balance each other's deficiencies, complement each other's strengths, and thus fulfill God's design for Biblical marriage. (Men should read my husband's book, *What the Bible Says About ... Being a Man*.)

CHAPTER IX

WOMAN – A VERY INFLUENCIAL PERSON

Some people believe that a woman's role as helpmate prevents her from being a significant force in society. Quite the opposite is actually true. In fact, a woman's influence is so powerful that she should be required to wear a **Warning!** label. In one way or another, every woman makes an impact on her man, her children, and the society in which she lives. Her influence is either beneficial (fulfilling the plan of God) or destructive (supporting the plan of Satan). This chapter reveals several areas in which a woman exerts either positive or negative influence. The material that is presented in this chapter should dispel the myth that the woman's submissive role is insignificant. It will also warn of the considerable damage that can be caused when a woman chooses to live outside God's design.

A Woman's Influence on Her Children

A well-known adage is, "The hand that rocks the cradle rules the world." Until quite recently, mother and the home were virtually synonymous in the minds of people. Memories of the childhood home usually centered on Mom – how she cooked, soothed pain, and especially the moral standards that she taught. A mother's influence over her children's attitudes about themselves and others, about authorities, and about God lasts a lifetime. In the Word of God a king instructs his son to heed his mother's instruction.

My son, hear the instruction of thy father, and
forsake not the law of thy mother: (Proverbs 1:8).

The above verse also states that the mother's teaching of children has equal standing with the father's. That teaching becomes the standard by which a new generation will live.

Most Christians today are deeply saddened by our nation's departure from God's Word and from basic morality. It is not coincidental that this decline in morality began after a large percentage of mothers entered the workplace. As a result of working outside the home, many of today's Christian mothers have abdicated their child-training responsibilities to secular daycare centers and public schools.

The secular world teaches its own standards and in many cases those standards are in direct opposition to Christian principles. This situation is producing an atmosphere fertile for immorality, such as providing children with condoms and teaching safe-sex as an alternative to self-discipline. While the secular world now rocks the cradle, absentee mothers are losing daily opportunities for the moral training of their children.

Deterioration of moral standards in our nation began with the neglect by Christian parents to properly train past generations. Restoration of morality can begin only when Christian parents return to the responsibility of training their own children. Christian women who love God more than the world can provide a home environment where the laws of God flourish and where satanic influence is exposed and countered.

I personally believe that every woman who understands Biblical principles can begin with her own children; and by training them in those standards can influence the revival of an entire nation. It is possible that at this very moment a Christian mother is molding the values of a future statesman, pastor, missionary, or honest auto mechanic. She is a living example of Biblical womanhood for her daughters to imitate when they are wives and mothers. In addition, she and her husband may be training their sons to be real men who value, respect, and protect women. No matter what the children's future may hold, their parents are actively implanting the qualities of godly character in their souls. The children's race, economic status, or intelligence are not as important as the lessons of self-discipline, honesty, trustworthiness, moral strength, courage, and respect for others that they are learning from their parents.

A Woman's Influence as a Teacher of Other Women

An influence that is desperately needed today is older women teaching younger women. For several generations the teaching of Biblical womanhood to our daughters has been seriously neglected in Christian homes and in our churches. One reason for this neglect has been due to women who are ignorant of Biblical principles themselves. Another reason is because many mothers today pursue personal ambitions outside the home and have no interest in training their daughters. The only marriage training most of our modern daughters ever receive is in their school home economics and sex education courses, from pulp magazines and the entertainment media, and from their peers. The emphasis of school courses and the entertainment media is primarily controlled by secular thought and includes no Biblical principles whatsoever. Likewise, a young woman's peers are usually as ignorant of Biblical principles as she is herself and can offer only youthful, self-centered advice.

God's purpose in commanding the older women to teach the younger women is ...*that the Word of God be not blasphemed* through the younger women's manner of life (Titus 2:5b). But today the Word of God *is* being blasphemed because many adult daughters follow secular opinions about life and marriage, rather than looking to the Word of God. This secular counsel encourages them to live in ways that directly oppose the Word of God, including immoral lifestyles and divorce on demand.

Marriage difficulties and divorce cause immense pain for everyone concerned – the husband, the wife, but especially the children. Many churches today are responding to this intense human agony by offering codependency programs and other psychologically based classes to try to deal with the aftermath of parents who have selfishly abandoned God's design for marriage. Unfortunately, these questionable solutions are similar to treating the symptoms of an illness, rather than eliminating the cause of the disease. God's method of having older women teaching younger women is a preventative measure that helps to keep the patients healthy, thereby preventing serious epidemics. Churches would help Christian marriages most by identifying and developing qualified older women to teach younger women about Biblical womanhood before the problems begin.

God has given the Biblical criteria by which we can identify the qualified older woman. Before she is allowed to teach, the older woman's life-resume should reflect the following attributes and qualifications:

> *The aged women likewise, that they be in behaviour as becometh holiness, not false accusers, not given to much wine, teachers of good things;* (Titus 2:3).

The "good things" that are to be taught include teaching younger women:

> ... *to be sober, to love their husbands, to love*
> *their children, To be discreet, chaste, keepers at*
> *home, good, obedient to their own husbands, that*
> *the word of God be not blasphemed* (Titus 2:4-5).

As a child of God, you should evaluate any woman who teaches you by these Biblical standards. Does her teaching reflect the "good things" of Titus 2:4-5? Does she honor or blaspheme the Word of God in her own life? If you follow her suggestions will they cause a growth of love and understanding between you and your husband, or will they increase alienation and cause dissension? Subjecting our modern "experts" to this close scrutiny will disqualify a great many of them (even some claiming to be Christians), thereby diminishing the harm that could be inflicted by their blasphemous advice.

A Woman's Influence Over Her Husband

As we have seen a woman can be a substantial influence on her children and on younger women. However, perhaps the greatest impact a woman makes is on her husband – the father of her children. A wife's influence is felt in four basic areas of her husband's life: his masculinity, his initiative, his leadership, and his spiritual life.

Her Husband's Masculinity

One Saturday morning a husband and wife in my neighborhood were holding a garage sale. People were walking around looking at the items for sale while the husband talked to a friend. A customer approached the husband and made a lowered bid for an end table. Upon overhearing her husband agree to the ten-dollar reduction, the wife called across the yard,

"What did you sell that for? Oh Jim, how idiotic!" Jim looked at his friend and shrugged his shoulders in embarrassment. If this scene had been in a movie, some appropriate music would have signaled that this was a significant moment. As it was, I may have been the only one who heard the death march for Jim's masculinity.

Without realizing that her words cut like a chisel, the wife at the garage sale chipped off a piece of her husband's manhood. Unknowingly, she helped her husband to lose interest in making further decisions. Jim most likely played it safe for the remainder of the day and deferred all questions to his wife. He may have eventually gone indoors to watch TV and left her to manage on her own. By the time she closed the garage sale, the wife probably felt totally exhausted and exasperated because she had to do everything herself. Jim's wife unwisely defeated her purpose of being a helpmate when she shamed her husband. Instead of encouraging him to make decisions, she helped him to retreat from decision-making. I wonder if the loss of ten dollars was worth the long-ranged damage to Jim's manhood?

The situation at the garage sale happened fifteen years ago. Since then the marriage climate has worsened even more in America. I hear the same type of emasculating treatment of husbands by their wives almost everywhere I go – including at church. Sadly, this is all too typical of the negative influence many modern wives inflict upon their husbands' manhood. The unbiblical wife is usually unaware that she can mentally and emotionally abuse her husband's masculinity when she treats him as a child, constantly complains about what a bad husband he is, or admonishes him in public. This type of wife frequently blames her husband for the weaknesses that she reinforces with her own words and actions. Rarely does a wife realize that the quality of her husband's leadership is directly proportional to the health of his manhood. Damage a husband's manhood and he will begin to lose the confidence, and often the desire, to be a responsible husband. Conversely, protect and support his manhood and he is encouraged to be a better leader, provider, and protector.

Her Husband's Initiative

It is not a misnomer when some husbands proudly refer to their wives as their "better half." A husband with this attitude is aware that his wife's influence adds to his life a previously missing ingredient. Without her he would have less reason to bear up under the hardships and burdens of a man's responsibility. Her demonstration of trust in his ability to succeed and her appreciation of his efforts strengthen his resolve to be victorious in life's battles. The Biblical woman is her husband's supportive half (not his "better half") as well as his loyal and compassionate friend.

On the other hand, the wife who refuses to fulfill the intended design of helpmate abandons her husband to fight his battles alone. Without a helpmate willing to fit with him, he is vulnerable to a multitude of difficulties. He needs his helpmate to help ease the pain in his life, but the unbiblical wife's indifference increases his suffering. Instead of building his confidence, her lack of support weakens his morale. Rather than assuaging any misgivings about his ability to lead and provide for his family, her distrustful criticisms increase his insecurity and destroy his initiative. When a wife is a negative influence on her husband, she becomes the "old ball and chain," rather than his supportive half.

Her Husband's Leadership

Some women become very confused concerning decision-making. They think that the husband must make every decision while the wife remains completely silent. Let me clear up this misconception.

It is true that God ordained the husband as the head of the family and that includes being responsible for major decisions that affect his family. However, this does not mean that the wife is never involved in any decision-making. There are two types of decisions that must be made concerning family living. Before we look at a woman's influence on her husband's leadership, let's first establish the difference between these two types of decision-making.

The first type of decision-making involves *leadership decisions*. The husband is responsible to God to oversee all issues that have a major impact on the entire family. A matter that requires a final determination before action can take place and policy making are within the realm of a husband's leadership. Examples of decisions that a husband should make are: determining where the family should live, where they attend church, decisions about job changes, establishing a budget, and setting the standards for child training. These examples are all within the husband's role and area of responsibility as leader, protector, and provider of his family

The second type of decision-making involves *supportive decisions* that follow through and successfully implement the policies of the leader, while remaining within the established guidelines. Examples of a wife's decisions are: finding ways to live within the budget, and actually training the children within the standards set. As long as the wife's decisions are within the guidelines set by her husband, she has tremendous freedom of choice. For instance, setting the family food budget is a policy decision, but planning the menus and determining where to find the best prices are decisions within the realm of supportive follow-through. A wife may need to seek her husband's approval before purchasing a major appliance, but she should not need to check with him before purchasing a head of lettuce.

Even though a husband is ultimately responsible for all leadership type of decisions, a wife should remember that she is always in a position to influence those decisions. A wife who knows her husband is secure about his role as leader may freely express her views, preferences, and insights during pre-decision discussions. The wife of a husband, who Biblically leads his family, can relax in the knowledge that her husband will weigh her ideas carefully before imposing a major policy for the family. Sadly, few wives today have reason to be confident in their husband's ability to make wise decisions. Therefore, it is a common belief that a wife should exert the strongest possible influence when she believes her husband's leadership is unwise or weak. However, this belief is counterproductive to the correct role of helpmate and only assures the continuation of poor leadership.

Dangerous Influences

Every wife influences her husband's life – either beneficially or harmfully. In order to assure that her influence is constructive, a wife must understand the power she has over her husband, especially one who is insecure about his leadership position. For instance, a persuasive wife is in danger of misusing her power to influence if her husband is less assertive than she. A discerning wife, who knows her husband might prefer to escape leadership responsibilities, should be especially careful to refrain from forcefully expressing her opinions. This is particularly true if she has a tendency to instigate debates over every decision, or if she finds that her husband is easily overpowered by her lengthy arguments. (The ability to out-talk a man does not mean a woman's opinions are correct.) When a woman uses her powers of persuasion consistently to talk her husband out of taking his place as leader, she discourages him from developing his full potential and can encourage him to become inactive as a leader. Many modern-day husbands have been persuaded to become silent partners in their marriages by these non-Biblical wives.

I realize that many women will feel frustrated at the idea of withholding their opinions from their less assertive husbands. "I cannot just keep my mouth shut and play like I am stupid," is how a great many women express their rejection of this concept. Before you throw out the whole concept, however, please consider that Rebekah, Isaac's wife, probably felt this way too.

The Bible tells us that while she was pregnant with twins, God told Rebekah that the elder son, Esau, would serve the younger son, Jacob. This promise was opposite the normal system of family leadership by the eldest son after the father's death. Additionally, Isaac favored Esau. Because of these apparent problems, Rebekah did not believe she could trust God to fulfill that which He had promised. She thought she personally *had* to make sure God's prophecy came true – even if she had to use deception to achieve her goal. Therefore, she urged her favorite son, Jacob, to deceive his father in order to steal his brother's blessing (Genesis 27:1-40). The results of Rebekah's influence were disastrous to the family. Esau was filled with jealous hatred for his brother (Genesis 24:41 and 28:6-9), and Jacob had to flee the country to escape his brother's wrath (Genesis 27:42-45). It is quite possible that Rebekah's interference caused her never to see her favorite son again!

When solutions to problems appear to take forever, a woman must be especially careful of her power to influence her husband. A woman typically wants decisions made and problems solved – NOW! When problems loom and solutions are not forthcoming, it is not unusual for a woman to become quite impatient. But, if she attempts to force her husband into a premature action she could easily create a disastrous situation.

Abraham's wife, Sara, is a perfect illustration of a wife who became impatient while waiting for something to happen. Sara was convinced that she was barren forever, so she suggested that Abraham should have a child by her handmaiden Hagar, in order to fulfill God's prophecy. Sara, like Rebekah, thought God's plan required her intervention. The consequences that fell upon their household when Abraham followed his wife's leadership are recorded in Genesis 16 and 21:9-21. Rebekah's and Sara's interfering influence over their husbands should prove that it is prudent for a wife to be concerned about the possible long-ranged effect of her suggestions – before she speaks.

Beneficial Influences

Whether your husband is nonassertive, assertive, or somewhere in between, the one guideline that will help you keep from exercising incorrect influence on him is your faith in God. Do you truly believe that God designed Biblical submission for your entire families benefit? Do you believe that He is in control? If so, you will want to operate according to God's plan for marriage.

As long as a wife is not argumentative (repetitive debating), resistive (refusing to accept her husband's final decision), or rebellious (defiant and insubordinate), she can speak her opinions (once, not thrice) during the decision making process. During these discussions a wife's submissive attitude should always be evident. She should only present her objections, or insights into possible problems, to the extent that she has fully communicated them. Her husband should never be caused to doubt her willingness to abide by his final decision.

Please do not fall for the popular misconception that a woman's submissive role leaves her weak and defenseless. Since it is God's design that a wife should submit to her husband, there is considerable power backing up her Biblical submission.

This does not mean that God will always prevent a husband from making leadership errors. God often uses a husband's error in judgment as a training exercise to improve his leadership in the future. A wife can relax in the knowledge that God will provide for her while He is training her husband. In addition, she should consider that while God is training her husband, He also desires for her to develop self-control, patience, and trust. In addition, she has the opportunity to manifest the fruit of the Spirit in her own life: *But the fruit of the Spirit is love, joy, peace, longsuffering, gentleness, goodness, faith, meekness, temperance*: (Galatians 5:22-23a). Such goals for her own life are more important than the temporary consequences of her husband's error in judgment.

Therefore, it is not the submissive wife who is defenseless; it is the non-submissive wife who is without defense. Within God's well-fortified citadel of Biblical marriage, a submissive wife is provided for today, as well as tomorrow.

Her Husband's Spiritual Life

More women attend church, read Christian books, teach Sunday school, and ask spiritual questions, than do men. Why, then, does God say, *And if they* (wives) *will learn anything, let them ask their own husbands at home* ... (1 Corinthians 14:35a) (Comment added)

When the serpent approached Eve, it was not because she was less spiritual than Adam, but because she was more emotionally responsive to misdirection. A modern woman's susceptibility to misdirection is the same as Eve's, no matter how logical or brilliant she may be. Remember, a woman's weaknesses are pride of knowledge that would make her like a god, and an insatiable desire to control the man; both of which cause her to be easily deceived. The husband's responsibility for spiritual leadership is a grace gift given by God for the wife's protection from deception.

By God's design the husband is the spiritual head of his family. However, his wife has a direct and powerful influence on his leadership. A woman who is more eager for spiritual information than her husband should not nag or try to push him into studying the Word of God. She is never to usurp his leadership position, nor is she to be his teacher:

> *Let the woman learn in silence with all subjection. But I suffer not a woman to teach, nor to usurp authority over the man, but to be in silence* (1 Timothy 2:11-12).

A wife is to ask her husband questions and then be attentive to his reply, trusting that God will supply the answers she needs. God can reward the Biblical wife's obedience to His Word by using her positive example as a powerful spiritual influence on her husband. This simple method is how God can use a Biblical wife to encourage and strengthen her husband in his spiritual leadership.

> *Likewise, ye wives, be in subjection to your own husbands; that, if any obey not the word, they also may without the word be won by the conversation of the wives; While they behold your chaste conversation coupled with fear* (1 Peter 3:1-2). (The fear referred to in context is of God, not a fear of husbands.)

Concern about their husband's poor leadership skills often prompts women to disobey God's design for marriage, especially in the area of spiritual leadership. However, no woman has more power to protect herself from the consequences of poor leadership than does God. Nor does any woman possess God's ability to weave together *all things* (Romans 8:28) into results that are beneficial for all those involved. Trusting God enough to obey Him makes a woman the recipient of an invincible heavenly advocate. A woman who insists on trying to protect herself by influencing her husband unwisely cuts off this unshakable power.

> *For after this manner in the old time the holy*
> *women also, who **trusted in God**, adorned*
> *themselves, being in subjection unto their own*
> *husbands: Even as Sara obeyed Abraham,*
> *calling him lord: whose daughters ye are, as*
> *long as ye do well, and are not afraid with any*
> *amazement* (1 Peter 3:5-6). (Emphasis added.)

The Greek word translated "afraid" in the verse above is
phobeo. Its meaning is "to frighten, or be alarmed." The Greek
word translated "amazement" means alarm or terrifying. An
expanded translation of 1 Peter 3:6 would emphasize the extent
to which Sarah is an example of a woman following her
husband's leadership.

> *Even as Sarah obeyed* (listened attentively and
> heeded the command or authority of) *Abraham,*
> *calling him lord:* (her authority) *whose*
> *daughters ye are, as long as ye do well, and are*
> *not **phobeo*** (frightened or alarmed) *with any*
> ***ptoesis*** (terror).(*Comments added)*

These verses promise that a wife does not need to fear the
results of her husband's decisions – even when they are wrong.
A woman who understands these principles realizes that her
influence is spiritually strongest when it is personally weakest.

A Final Warning!

Many of today's women feel personally insulted when they
are taught that their husbands are to be the spiritual heads of
their families. These women usually declare themselves
independent of their husbands. The results of this stance are
disastrous to the women, to their husbands, and to their families.

A woman who believes that her own intellect can protect
her from deception is deceived already. There is no intellect
great enough to declare itself exempt from God's Word, plan,
or design. A woman deceived into believing that she is superior

to God's design will inevitably become a prideful woman – rebellious to all authority and arrogant in her knowledge of Biblical data. ...*we know that we all have knowledge. Knowledge puffeth up, but charity edifieth* (1 Corinthians 8:1b).

A proud, self-righteous woman often becomes the wife who uses her religion as a weapon. She "preaches" at her husband and showers him with condemnation for his many sins. When a wife becomes proud in her own supposed spiritual autonomy, her husband's resolve to improve his spiritual knowledge may be weakened. It is easier for him to "save face" by pretending not to care about spiritual things, than to compete with a wife who uses her vast vocabulary and apparent knowledge of Biblical facts as a club over his head. When his confidence in himself is shattered, he is less interested in protecting his wife from false teachings (she would not listen anyway). Furthermore, this husband will frequently take no interest in church, maintaining that it is for women and children only. A preponderance of women as spiritual leaders of their families causes the church to suffer from a lack of male leadership. Sadly, this type of wife often wishes that she could influence her husband toward spiritual matters, completely unaware that she is his excuse to default from his responsibility as spiritual head of the family.

In Conclusion

To be certain that her influence is beneficial to those she loves, a Biblical woman must practice discernment and employ wisdom. Among her standards of conduct should be self-control and avoidance of manipulative tactics. A Biblical woman knows that a self-important image is not a Christ-like image; therefore, she submits herself to God's will.

There are many benefits when a Biblical helpmate influences her husband positively. Freedom from competition for the headship position at home makes a husband a more confident employee in the workplace. His desire to lead well promotes a desire for self-improvement. The husband who has a Biblical helpmate will often begin to develop his potential for leadership and for service in the church. As a result, he and his wife become an excellent Christian testimony, which glorifies God and prevents His Word from being blasphemed. This couple's unity provides their children with a stable and secure home environment. Furthermore, because God protects those who honor Him, the whole nation benefits from Biblically functioning homes. At the very least, children are reared to be good citizens and do not participate in further destroying the morality of the society in which they live. All these blessings are possible when a woman trusts God enough to function as a Biblical wife and to allow Him to influence her husband in ways that bring glory and honor to Him.

CHAPTER X

A ROLE MODEL FOR BIBLICAL WOMANHOOD

I have attempted to present some basic principles for Biblical womanhood in the previous nine chapters of this book. Proverbs 31:10-31 can be said to be the condensed version of those principles; and the woman described there is the epitome of Biblical womanhood. As we come to the close of **Section One: Foundations**, it seems fitting to introduce the woman who has been the Biblical woman's role model for thousands of years.

Unfortunately, many woman treat the Proverbs 31 woman as a relic of the past – ideal perhaps, but certainly unrealistic for the complexities of modern living. Even among Christian women the consensus of today's thinking is that: it is no longer practical for a woman to trust her physical, mental, emotional, and financial well-being to the same life-style that this woman represents. I exhort the Christian woman to remember that the faithfulness of God's Word dictates that Proverbs 31 is as relevant today as it was the day it was written.

Heaven and earth shall pass away, but my
words shall not pass away (Matthew 24:35).

Christian women can still look confidently at the Proverbs 31 woman as their role model. The following is a hypothetical interview in which the Proverbs 31 woman is asked some questions about issues that pressure women today. Her responses are paraphrased, but the verses that relate to her answers are in parentheses so you may confirm their accuracy.

Modern Questions for the Proverbs 31 Woman

1. Do you feel your talents are smothered because you are to be submissive to your husband's leadership?

"No, I do my work willingly (not grudgingly)" (verse 13). "I am satisfied and fulfilled for I sense that my gain is good" (verse 18). "I have strength and dignity and smile (have no fear) at the future" (verses 21 & 25). "All that I do shows my willingness to be of service to my household and others" (verses 15, 16, 18-22, 24, 27-31).

2. Do you feel that you have lost all personal identity and have become merely an extension of your husband?

"No, I am worth far more than jewels" (verse 10). "I am strong" (verse 17). "I have compassion" (verse 20). "I am wise and kind" (verse 26). "Strength and dignity are part of my character and my family's future is secure" (verses 11 & 25). "I am praised, honored, and respected by my children and my husband" (verse 28). "My husband considers me the most wonderful woman in the world" (verse 29).

3. Have you stifled your own personality and neglected the development of your own intelligence through mindless drudgery?

"No, not at all. I have a very keen business sense" (verses 13-24). "When I speak, it is with wisdom. I teach kindness. My soul is exposed by what and how I speak" (verse 26). "I use my intelligence to serve my household well" (verses 15, 16, 18-22, 27-31).

4. Are you just a lady of leisure – lazy, kept, spending your time watching soap operas on television, doing useless chores, instead of accomplishing something of value for society?

"What a strange question! I am not a burden to my husband because my deeds cause him only good and not evil" (i.e. not an embarrassment to him, do not cause him misery, distress, injury, or wrong) (verse 12). "I am a hard worker. I serve my children and my husband. I also serve my community" (verses 13-22, 24, 25, 27). "My husband does not need to worry about what is happening at home. He can trust me and attend to his business. Because I do my job he lacks nothing" (verse 11). "I delight in my work" (verse 13). "I produce by service (the hands) and I am praised in the city" (verse 31). How is this not valuable to the society in which I live?

5. Do you feel the need to leave those boring, repetitive, futile domestic chores to become a complete, valuable person? Should you think of the future and what might happen if you suddenly had to support yourself?

> "Absolutely not! My trust is in God, not in
> myself. I support my husband and do my part
> within the boundaries of my role" (All verses).
> "Together we prosper and are praiseworthy"
> (verses 23 &31). "The underlying motive of all
> that I do is service for others, not self-service"
> (verses 11, 12, 23, 28, & 29). "Because I do the
> will of the Lord I do not feel insecure, fearful,
> or in need of protecting myself" (verses 18, 21,
> 25, & 31).

Proverbs 31 is a declaration that there is no higher calling for a woman than that of wife and mother. The Proverbs 31 woman also had the freedom to develop business interests. These interests did not interfere with her main roles as helpmate to her husband, mother of her children, and keeper of their home. All her activities were interrelated with her home, and they were extensions of her role as a Biblical woman. The Proverbs 31 woman's motivations and accomplishments reflected the revealed will of God for womanhood. She is the forerunner of Biblical womanhood and her example exhorts generations of believing women to follow her lead.

Throughout history other women have chosen different paths and have even been lauded as role models for younger generations. Many have achieved fame and fortune, only to find that their achievements are void of fulfillment. Remarks that a famous movie star made during her lifetime describe just such emptiness. A newspaper printed the following statements on the day following Ava Gardner's death:

> Ava Gardner speaks out: "I act for money, no
> other reason. Since I made my first picture in
> 1941, I have not done a thing that is worthwhile."
> "I have never enjoyed making films, and I do

not like being a so called film star. I have not
the emotional make-up for it, nor the love of
exhibitionism. I am much too shy." Gardner
once said she grew up hoping to find "one good
man I could love and marry and cook for and
make a home for, who would stick around for
the rest of my life. I never found him. If I had,
I would have traded my career in a minute."[11]

I feel an overwhelming sadness when reading Ava Gardner's
assessment of her life. Her expression of emptiness and lack
of fulfillment stands in sharp contrast to the fullness of the life
of the Proverbs 31 woman. Gardner would have forsaken all
her achievements for what any Biblical woman has. It is too
late for her, but perhaps her words will help warn other women
– before they suffer the same type of loss and before the end of
their lives reflect the same despair.

A woman who devotes her life to living Biblical womanhood
chooses the most important career that any woman can possibly
pursue. The Biblical woman is the only one who can support
her husband, and so encourage him to be everything God intends
for him to be. A Biblical wife, by her submission, can be a
testimony of Christ's selfless sacrifice in His submission to the
plan of God the Father. Her success as a Biblical wife is a
confirmation of God's provision, and her submission in marriage
is a picture of the church's relationship to Christ. Her dedication
to her family, guided by her knowledge of the principles of
Biblical womanhood, will provide the stability her children need
as preparation for meeting the challenges of adulthood. A
woman can search to the ends of the earth for a way to serve
God, but she will never find a higher calling, or a more fulfilling
one, than that of helpmate to her own husband.

CHAPTER XI

PUTTING IT ALL TOGETHER

Our study of Biblical womanhood to this point has established a firm foundation of Biblical principles on which to build a marriage. We have seen how the woman was created as one-half of the original creation that God named "mankind." The woman and the man are incomplete without each other (except for the specialized exception of celibacy. 1 Corinthians 7:7). We have discovered that God's purpose for the woman is to be a helpmate (aide, assistant, supporter, backer, etc.) to her man. We have been reminded that she was made from the man for the man – not merely for the man's pleasure, but for the fulfillment of God's plan for mankind. The woman was created after the man, but this does not mean that she is second best. Woman is a special, and a specialized, creation. She is to be the mate and creative helper of her husband. As life-giver and nurturer of their children, the woman also plays a specific role in the divine directive to mankind to populate the earth.

Why, then, have so many women today rejected this grand design? Deception! The Bible says that in the last days people will be ...*without natural affection* (2 Timothy 3:3). They will be self-centered and unloving. Can you think of any better example of this lack of natural affection than the increasing number of women today who are not only leaving their husbands to follow their own dreams, but who are also abandoning their children? It is as if these women have been bewitched away from their devotion to family. The truth is that Satan has been as successful in the mass deception of modern-day women as he was with Eve in the garden. He has appealed to the woman's lust for acquisition of knowledge and to her prideful desire to rule her man – and the woman has fallen again; taking her family with her. Through all forms of the entertainment media Satan *constantly* bombards today's women with his party line.

"Knowledge equals freedom."

"Be your own authority."

"Women are superior to men."

"You do not need a man to tell you what to do."

"You are being kept from good things by men."

As went Eve, so goes an ever-increasing number of modern-day women, including far too many Christian women. Love of self is encouraged more than love of God and His Word. Young women today are surrounded by the promotion of vain and self-centered ambition more than purity and self-less service.

We have studied the consequences of Eve's fall on all women – great difficulty in child bearing and a strong desire to control her man. And, apparently worst of all, the husband was given authority over the wife. Consequently, the one who desired to be autonomous even from God must now submit to another mere human. These consequences could all add up to be an almost unbearable curse for Eve and her daughters if it were not for God's grace.

Mankind could not survive the consequences of its sin but for the fact that God is love, not just justice. In His grace, His plan provides bountiful blessings for the wife through her husband's position of leadership. Her husband is to provide vision for the marriage, he is to shield her from deception and protect her physically, and he is to provide for her and their children, as well as cherish her for life. She, in turn, can enjoy oneness of soul with her husband, a personal sense of security, and a feeling of fulfillment, when she follows God's plan and trusts Him with her life.

We have also studied the most difficult concept for willful creatures to accept – authority. All of mankind would find life easier, if they understood and trusted God's provision of human authority. Proper authority provides structure, order, safety, peace, and maximum freedom for the individual. A wife can trust her husband's leadership because of her knowledgeable trust in God, not because of mindless confidence in another fallible human being. Jesus Christ's submission to the Father's will is the supreme example for the Biblical wife's submission to her husband.

We have learned the crucial difference between submission and obedience. We found that a wife, on occasion, can obey her husband, but still not be submissive. We learned that the submission God expects from a Biblical wife, is the voluntary yielding of her will; it is not the unquestioning obedience expected of a child or a slave. We discovered that she is held to a higher standard than merely being obedient; a Biblical wife is accountable to God for her attitude and actions. "Submissive noncompliance" protects the Biblical wife from being pressured into sin by those over her.

We have also examined some of the unique factors that make the man so different from the woman. The major factor is the male ego. Rather than some horrible drive designed to dominate women, this ego is found to be essential to proper manliness, but it is also very fragile. The Biblical woman will become an expert in her man's ego – how not to harm it, and how properly to encourage his manhood. Understanding the necessity of the legitimate male ego, with all its drives and functions, is one of the first steps to becoming a supportive helpmate.

If the male ego was not a major enough difference between men and women, we also learned that men think differently than women. The man is objective and data-oriented in his thinking, while the woman thinks in terms of relationships, emotions, and pictures. Incompatible as these two may appear to be, they merge in a mature marriage to produce a balanced viewpoint in all areas of life. A marriage is like two interlocking parts of a puzzle. Apart, the parts are incomplete but together they combine to produce a whole that is greater than its parts.

Next, we discovered the tremendous influence every woman has over those around her. Her influence can either be beneficial or destructive to other women, to her children, and especially to her husband. We studied the four main areas where a woman influences her husband, either positively or negatively. These areas are: his masculinity, his initiative, his leadership, and his spiritual life. It is easy to see that a woman does not need to exert herself forcefully in order to make her mark upon the world. In fact, she may need to restrain herself in order to make the best contribution.

Finally, we have seen the spiritual and earthly importance that God designed for Biblical womanhood. The woman is not only important to her husband, she is crucial to her children and can be a positive testimony to all those around her. She can also express her creativity and find great fulfillment in her unique role. The final conclusion can only be that Biblical womanhood is indeed a woman's highest calling.

SECTION II

OPPOSITIONS TO BIBLICAL WOMANHOOD

INTRODUCTION

Section One set forth the Biblical position on womanhood and marriage. Christians, both men and women, were once taught many of these same principles about family living in their churches. As these Christians believed and lived what they were taught; they influenced the society in which they lived.

Tragically, Biblical teaching about male and female roles and parenting is either neglected or abandoned in many churches today. This departure from teaching family living from God's Word leaves whole congregations vulnerable to their own imaginations and the influences of humanistic philosophies. Now, instead of Christians influencing society; society influences Christians. While humanistic values prevail, God's standards are treated as relics of the past. As a result, it is increasingly difficult to observe any difference between how believers and unbelievers live their lives.

> *Salt is good: but if the salt have lost his savour, wherewith shall it be seasoned? It is neither fit for the land, nor yet for the dunghill; but men cast it out. He that hath ears to hear, let him hear* (Luke 14:34-35).

The consequences of abandoning God's design for men and women have been catastrophic to all. The damage can now be seen as divorce and sexual immorality wreak havoc on our present and future generations. What is so heartbreaking to me is that some pastors today have privately agreed with the material in this book and my husband's books, but still refuse to instruct their people about God's plan for families. They fear a negative reaction from the women in their congregation who have fallen, like Eve, for satanic deception; and from the reverberation of their husbands who, like Adam, followed her lead.

This section, **Oppositions to Biblical Womanhood,** will not attempt to cover *why* pastors began to neglect, or explain away, Scriptures about the male and female role. Instead, we will cover two reasons why so many modern women revolt whenever Bible teachers *do* teach the subject. It is my prayer that if the reader understands why some women *choose* to live their lives in opposition to God's design for womanhood, she will be spared from joining their revolt. Also, it is my prayer that enough Christian women will return to God's design in their marriages and that they will become like healing salt to a dying nation.

Oppositions to Biblical Woman is designed to alert women to the anti-Biblical position of today's vain (empty, deceitful) philosophies concerning women. It is also designed to reveal how Satan attempts to implement his war against God by using humans. This section will help to identify the lies that can lead women into vain philosophies and reveal to the reader how their effect can be defused.

This section will also analyze several faulty thinking patterns that block women from the truth about womanhood and reveal how the reader can replace humanistic foolishness with God's wisdom. Understanding the concepts presented in **Section II** can help protect a woman from being used by Satan or from being controlled by her own sin nature.

CHAPTER XII

VAIN PHILOSOPHIES

Vanity of vanities, saith the Preacher, vanity of vanities; all is vanity (Ecclesiastes 1:2).

The thing that hath been, it is that which shall be; and that which is done is that which shall be done: and there is no new thing under the sun (Ecclesiastes 1:9).

There is nothing new under the sun! All of the "new" humanistic philosophies that attempt to explain who we are and how we should live are simply modern versions of the old counterfeit philosophy with which Satan deceived Eve. Men and women have always had to choose between God's revealed Word and Satan's counterfeit philosophies. Each human being, from Adam and Eve to you, must choose which philosophy they will listen to and follow.

How to Identify Satanic Philosophies

Beware lest any man spoil you through philosophy and vain deceit, after the tradition

>*of men, after the rudiments of the world, and*
>*not after Christ* (Colossians 2:8).

There is only one *true* philosophy of life and; it is revealed by the Word of God. However, there are *many* false philosophies. The believer in Christ needs to realize that every viewpoint about life that does not come from God ultimately comes from Satan. Satan rejected God and declared war against Him, thus establishing the basis for all vain philosophies. Satan attempted to use mankind as a tool in his warfare; and man fell for his evil manipulation. As it was in the beginning, so it is today – modern vain philosophies still reject God and His authority. Satan is still attempting to use mankind in his war against God. Whether it is humanism, feminism, or any other ism, vain philosophies endeavor to explain the meaning of life apart from God.

The human authors of anti-God philosophies are often considered by mankind to be original thinkers. However, like Satan, these human philosophers base their systems of thinking on the rejection of God and a denial of the absolute authority of His Word. When human philosophies reject God, their founders are not really being the brilliant original thinkers that they believe themselves to be. In reality, they are just following the vain philosophy founded by Satan – the father of lies.

Jesus told the religious leaders of His day that they were following the vain philosophy of Satan:

>*Why do ye not understand my speech? even*
>*because ye cannot hear my word. Ye are of your*
>*father the devil, and the lusts of your father ye will*
>*do. He was a murderer from the beginning, and*
>*abode not in the truth, because there is no truth in*
>*him. When he speaketh a lie, he speaketh of his*
>*own: for he is a liar, and the father of it*
>(John 8:43-44).

Vain philosophies can be identified in several ways. The most obvious sign is a beginning premise that rejects God. But the knowledgeable student of God's Word can also recognize the more subtly deceptive tenets. The basic doctrines of false philosophies follow the same pattern that Satan utilized when he deceived Eve in the garden. The pattern of many satanic philosophies begin by suggesting *doubt* that God's Word is literal and therefore they urge us to reject Biblical principles and standards. Vain philosophies also contain messages that emotionally incite us to feel *discontent* with the Biblical way of life. And finally, a satanic philosophy encourages its followers to live lifestyles of *disbelief* that are in direct rebellion against God and His Word.*

An Example of a Modern Vain Philosophy

An example of a teaching that follows the satanic pattern of thinking is the women's liberation movement, now known as the feminist movement. Sometime in the early 1970's this popular movement came to my attention and I asked myself, "Is this movement compatible with God's Word, or is it a deceitful philosophy conceived and promoted by Satan?"

A study of the authors and promoters of the feminist movement, along with a review of their basic philosophical tenets, immediately revealed the original source of this "new" thinking about women's roles. I discovered that, the feminist movement promotes *doubt* about God's way, *discontentment* with being a wife and mother, and *disbelief* about God's order

---

* I am indebted to Pastor Carl Denti for this insight. He is the teacher whose Bible research discovered that Satan's philosophy consists of a sophisticated structure that first causes *doubt*, then leads to *discontentment*, and finally leads to *disbelief* or rebellion.

for marriage and the family. The following are just a few of the many statements by the leaders and promoters of the feminist movement that demonstrate the anti-God origin of this vain philosophy.

Paul Kurtz, Professor Emeritus of Philosophy at the State University of New York in Buffalo, founder and chairman of the Council for Secular Humanism and Prometheus Books (Humanism's most influential publishing house), author of the *Humanist Manifesto II*, and editor-in chief of *Free Inquiry* magazine. He is also a former Co-President of the *International Humanist and Ethical Union and Humanist Laureate and President of the* International Academy of Humanism. Mr. Kurtz has said:

> "The feminist movement was begun and has been nourished by leading humanist women." [12]

Mr. Kurtz specifically mentions Elizabeth Cady Stanton, Betty Friedan (author of *The Feminine Mystique*, 1963, and Humanist of the Year 1975), Gloria Steinem, and Simone de Beauvoir. His acknowledgement that the feminist movement and humanism are philosophically linked is very important to note, because humanists emphatically reject God and they believe that mankind is its own God.

Julian Huxley (1888-1975), another well known humanist and evolutionist, defined a humanist as follows:

> "I use the word 'Humanist' to mean someone who believes that man is just as much a natural phenomenon as an animal or a plant, that his body, his mind, and his soul were not supernaturally created but are all products of evolution, and that he is not under the control or guidance of any supernatural Being or beings, but has to rely on himself and his own powers."[13]

Elizabeth Cady Stanton, 1815-1902, recognized by Mr. Paul Kurtz as a fellow humanist, was one of the leading organizers for the *Seneca Falls Declaration on Women's Rights*, July 19, 1948, and author of *Eighty Years and More* in 1898. She writes:
> "The memory of my own suffering has prevented me from ever shadowing one young soul with the superstitions of the Christian religion."[14]

Annie Laurie Gaylor, co-founder of the Freedom From Religion Foundation, editor of the book *Women Without Superstition: No God's; No Masters,* a very active atheist today, and a feminist writer in *The Humanist* (this is an official bimonthly magazine for humanist leader's articles) writes:
> "Let's forget about the mythical Jesus and look for encouagement, solace, and inspiration from real women... Two thousand years of patriarchal rule under the shadow of the cross ought to be enough to turn women toward the feminist 'salvation' of the world."[15]

Gloria Steinem, editor of *Ms. Magazine*, author of *Outrageous Acts and Everyday Rebellions* in which she admired Elizabeth Cady Stanton for her rejection of Biblical womanhood.[16] Ms. Steinem is a vocal leader in the present day feminist movement, who believes we should:
> "...raise our children to believe in human potential not God."[17]

Sol Gordon, another writer for *The Humanist* magazine said:
> "The traditional family, with all its supposed attributes, enslave woman, it reduced her to a breeder and caretaker of children, a servant to her spouse, a cleaning lady, and at times a victim of the labor market as well."[18]

True to the pattern of satanic doctrines, those who authored the humanistic and feminist movements promoted the rejection of God and His Word as the final authority about creation, womanhood, manhood, and marriage. Today, the proponents of feminism continue to express rejection that God's Word is to be taken literally. Furthermore, they persuade women who listen to their doctrines to become dissatisfied with a woman's God-given roles and functions in life. Feminists/humanists also advocate the replacement of God's truths with standards and lifestyles that directly oppose the Word of God. In fact, in order to be a true disciple of the feminist philosophy a woman must directly rebel against God, His plan, and His Word. This vain philosophy proposes to liberate women, but it does not; instead, it enslaves its misguided followers to Satan.

Why Christian Women Fall Prey to Feminist Philosophies

But I fear, lest by any means, as the serpent beguiled Eve through his subtilty, so your minds should be corrupted from the simplicity that is in Christ (2 Corinthians 11:3).

Even though God has faithfully warned Christians to be vigilant against the influences of Satan, many of our Christian contemporaries fall prey to the vain philosophy of feminism. Far too many Christian women today have been persuaded to reject their husband's role as head of the family, and they have been incited to be discontent with the honorable roles of wife, mother, and homemaker. Why have these anti-Biblical attitudes become acceptable to many of today's Christian women?

One reason Christian women are being deceived by this satanic doctrine is that their exposure to non-Biblical opinions about feminism is proportionately greater than their exposure to Biblical truths about womanhood. Virtually every American woman today is surrounded by information that is written by, or intended to appease, those who believe the philosophical viewpoint of feminism. My husband and I tested this theory one day when we paid close attention to just one of the many sources of information that is intended to influence our thinking and emotions – television commercials.

The first commercial depicted a man who was unable to make a decision about whether or not to buy the services of a certain long-distance telephone company. He turned the phone over to his wife and appealed to her for leadership. A later scene showed the husband (much relieved from the responsibility of making such a heavy decision) when he learned that his wife had finalized a contract with the telephone company for its services. This same type of scenario was repeated in other commercials for soup and credit cards.

Another commercial portrayed a wife who was instructing her inept husband on how to do the laundry; another showed a wife placating her child-like husband's sweet-tooth with a healthy treat. In another advertisement, a woman on an overnight business trip was calling home to her husband and child.

All of the commercials not only tried to sell their products, they were also selling subtle feminist messages to unwary viewers. They consistently portrayed the husbands as child-like and inept, while the wives were knowledgeable and in control of family leadership. Even more importantly, most of the commercials placed the husbands in a **reversal of roles.** These husbands were shown to be functioning as their wives' helpmates.

Messages promoting role reversal and other tenets of feminism are not found only in advertisements, and they are not always directed at women. Nearly all of our present-day information sources send subtle messages that are meant to inform, educate, and influence the thinking of every man, woman, and child with regard to male and female roles. The majority of news reports, television programs, movies, and written materials are saturated with slanted information designed to influence our thinking. This information is about such real concerns as: male and female roles in marriage and society, divorce, sexual conduct such as pre-marital sex or homosexuality, work in and out of the home, child-care, physical abuse, abortion, and sexual discrimination. In virtually every case this so-called educational material directly or indirectly opposes the Biblical philosophy of womanhood or the God-ordained roles for man and wife. The following paragraph from the *Arizona Republic* newspaper contains an example of how the message of *doubt, discontent, and disbelief* is being subtly expounded by the media.

> "Even just a generation ago, most wives had little opportunity for infidelity." (Is the author suggesting that these women were underprivileged?) "They were stuck" (implying reluctant confinement) "in their homes with their child and other hausfraus" (Name calling is also a common tactic) while their husbands went off to work, often among attractive coworkers." (Sowing the seeds of discontent through suspicion and jealousy is another common practice.) (Emphasis added.) [19]

In this one paragraph alone, several subliminal messages have been implanted. Negative words and phrases such as "little opportunity," "stuck," and "hausfraus," along with other catchwords and slogans, are used for their power to influence thought and emotions. And they almost always leave the female reader with negative feelings about her role as helpmate and mother. Long after a woman puts down her magazine or newspaper, these negative feelings will remain in her subconscious mind. Then, when her husband acts inconsiderately, when her child whines all day, when she feels unattractive, or when she feels unappreciated and frustrated because "a woman's work is never done," those embedded adverse emotions can surface.

Without even realizing that the source for her discontent is the subconscious exposure to propaganda designed to cause discontent, a woman is likely to begin applying negative thoughts and feelings to her own circumstances. She may think to herself; "I am stuck, I am nothing but a frumpy housewife. I need freedom to be myself." Future twisted messages about the supposed (or even real) mistreatment of women will reinforce her media-agitated emotions, causing her to feel that she is *personally* mistreated. Unconsciously indoctrinated by misleading information, errors, false teaching, and outright lies, this woman will then dwell on and magnify the small bumps in the road of marriage that she normally would not consider to be severe. This disastrous sequence of events, from complacency to discontent, may occur *not necessarily because of actual personal experiences*, but because of media-implanted seeds of discontent.

Countering Vain Philosophies

A woman cannot completely avoid being exposed to the many satanic philosophies of this world but she can counter their influence on her life. First, a Biblical woman should be constantly alert to the fact that most false philosophies will appeal to her emotions, her sense of "personal rights," her desire for autonomy, and her sin-nature weaknesses. Secondly, when a woman begins to recognize the intruding influence of deceptive philosophies on her thinking, she should do as our Lord Jesus Christ did when He was confronted and tempted by Satan. Christ countered the attempt of Satan to influence his thinking and prevent Him from His mission in life with the absolute truth of God's Word.

> *Then saith Jesus unto him, Get thee hence,*
> *Satan: for it is written, Thou shalt worship the*
> *Lord thy God, and him only shalt thou serve*
> (Matthew 4:10).

It is time for Christian women to stop being influenced by satanic doctrines that oppose the truth of God's Word. However, a woman is incapable to resist these influences with her own fleshly power.

> *For though we walk in the flesh, we do not war*
> *after the flesh: (For the weapons of our warfare*
> *are not carnal, but mighty through God to the*
> *pulling down of strong holds;)*
> (2 Corinthians 10:3-4).

Satan's forces are so strong in this modern world that the only sure weapon a woman has against satanic influence is in the mind of Christ. A woman who brings *into captivity every thought to the obedience of Christ* will be well equipped to make a distinction between God's truth and Satan's fiction.

> *Casting down imaginations, and every high*
> *thing that exalteth itself against the knowledge*
> *of God, and bringing into captivity every thought*
> *to the obedience of Christ;* (2 Corinthians 10:5).

God's Word contains all the knowledge that we need to live a full and satisfying life. It is in God's Word that a woman may correctly focus her desire for knowledge. The Bible will help her discover how to view herself in relation to God and to other people. It gives her specific rules and guidelines to follow throughout her life in every situation and every circumstance. It instructs each of us in the one and only true philosophy – God's viewpoint, and protects all those who will heed His truths against vain philosophies.

> *How sweet are thy words unto my taste! yea,*
> *sweeter than honey to my mouth! Through thy*
> *precepts I get understanding: therefore I hate*

every false way. Thy word is a lamp unto my feet, and a light unto my path
(Psalm 119:103-106).

Thy testimonies have I taken as an heritage for ever: for they are the rejoicing of my heart. I have inclined mine heart to perform thy statutes alway, even unto the end. I hate vain thoughts: but thy law do I love. Thou art my hiding place and my shield: I hope in thy word. Depart from me, ye evildoers: for I will keep the commandments of my God. Uphold me according unto thy word, that I may live: and let me not be ashamed of my hope. Hold thou me up, and I shall be safe: and I will have respect unto thy statutes continually
(Psalm 119:111-117).

CHAPTER XIII

FAULTY THINKING PATTERNS

Vain philosophies are not the only enemy to a woman's right thinking. Her own sin nature works through her will and emotions to produce strong personal opinions that also oppose God's Word. The faulty thinking patterns that result from these opinions make living Biblical womanhood almost impossible (if it were not for God's grace that is). This chapter will expose some of the types of faulty thinking patterns that are most common to women and will suggest how such erroneous thinking can be conquered.

A woman's thinking (like that of a man's) may appear to be intelligent, logical, or even lofty, but her thoughts and opinions are formed within a very limited and imperfect human mind and so they are subject to error. By contrast, God's thoughts are infinitely unlimited and completely free of error.

> *For my thoughts are not your thoughts, neither are your ways my ways, saith the LORD. For as the heavens are higher than the earth, so are my ways higher than your ways, and my thoughts than your thoughts* (Isaiah 55:8-9).

Whenever a woman hears Biblical truth that is contrary to one of her previously formed opinions, she faces a critical decision. In that moment, her faulty human thinking collides with divine truth and she is forced to make a choice. Will she adhere to her own opinions, or will she accept God's thoughts? Since God's thoughts are infinitely higher than human opinions, it seems only reasonable that a Christian woman would wish to trade upward. The verse below declares that our human thinking needs to be totally changed in order to understand God's will.

> *And be not conformed to this world: but be ye transformed by the renewing of your mind, that ye may prove what is that good, and acceptable, and perfect, will of God* (Romans 12:2).

The following are four common examples of faulty thinking that will be compared to the Word of God. You may see yourself in one or more of these examples. I realize that some of this information may be painful, but I hope you will not automatically ignore (or reject) any conviction you might feel as you work through these pages. Instead, pray for a receptive heart so that God can reveal to you any faulty thinking pattern you might have.

Selfish Thinking

A disheartened Christian marriage counselor once told my husband that the number one hindrance to the successful counseling of couples today is selfish thinking. He said that a large percentage of Christian couples who come to him for help actually only want their own way. They selfishly refuse to relinquish their personal demands in order to make their marriage work. These men and women stubbornly refuse any advice that would require them to sacrifice their own will. Selfish thinking exists in many Christians, even though a primary characteristic of Christianity is supposed to be the willingness to place others before self.

Let nothing be done through strife or vainglory;
but in lowliness of mind let each esteem other
better than themselves. Look not every man on
his own things, but every man also on the things
of others. Let this mind be in you, which was
also in Christ Jesus: (Philippians 2:3-5).

The mind (attitude) *which was also in Christ Jesus* was selflessness, manifested by His complete submission to God's will, *...not as I will, but as thou wilt* (Matthew 26:39b). Jesus did not regard Himself above God's plan nor did He consider His own interests greater than the needs of the people He came to save. The attitude Christ had toward His designed purpose is the same attitude Christian women should have toward living Biblical womanhood. Selfishness has no place in a Christian marriage. Stubborn demands, lack of consideration for her husband's best interest, or refusal to bow to God's will is exceedingly unbecoming to a Christian woman.

Judgmental Thinking

Marriage is *the* most intimate relationship that one person can have with another. Intimacy can be the means of a comfortable and enjoyable companionship between a husband and wife, or it can be the catalyst for judgmental attitudes. As the old adage so aptly states, "familiarity breeds contempt." This familiarity results from an intimate knowledge of a mate's sin nature weaknesses, which in turn can lead to judging.

Judging is a particular problem for many women, which causes them to be hypercritical of their husbands. A woman who has a problem with a judgmental attitude cannot stand to leave uncorrected any perceived wrongdoing. This is the ingrained mothering makeup of a woman – to teach what is right and to correct that which is wrong. Mothering is necessary for training small children, but when a wife applies teaching or training to her husband it is an invasion of his privacy as an adult and a lack of respect for him as her leader. The relationship between a wife and a husband was never meant to be that of mother and child. A woman should judge her own performance, but she has no right to demand perfection from her husband.

A husband's growth towards maturity can be severely hampered by a judgmental wife. His attention is drawn away from becoming aware of his need for change because he becomes focused on his wife's obviously judgmental attitude.

> *Let us not therefore judge one another any more: but judge this rather, that no man put a stumblingblock or an occasion to fall in his brother's way* (Romans 14:13).

Instead of judging her husband, a woman should concentrate on bringing her own attitudes and actions up to God's expectations. A Biblical woman will leave her husband in God's hands for Him to bring about any necessary changes.

> *Likewise, ye wives, be in subjection to your own husbands; that, if any obey not the word, they also may without the word be won by the conversation of the wives; While they behold your chaste conversation coupled with fear* (1 Peter 3:1-2).

Note: The first occurrence in this verse of "the word" refers to the Word of God, while the second refers to an absence of the wives' words. The Bible makes it very clear that God does not need a wife to be His spokesperson in order to correct her husband's actual (or supposed) wrongs.

Self-Righteous Thinking

A woman who indulges in judgmental thinking patterns almost always becomes very self-righteous as well. She is usually convinced that because she is "right," she must control the thoughts and actions of everyone around her in order to ensure their success or to prevent their failure.

As we saw in **Chapter IV**, the desire to control is a strong trait of every woman. We women are often portrayed in this negative manner in cartoons and jokes about women. The controlling woman who constantly criticizes her husband and the mother-in-law who interferes in her adult children's lives are easy targets for comedians. Sadly, the self-righteous, controlling woman is so real that many people have little difficulty in relating to these jokes.

Submission in marriage is extremely odious for the self-righteous woman. Because she cannot trust anyone else to be right other than her, she will fight for the decision-making position in almost any situation. A self-righteous woman will emphasize all the faults of her husband as her excuse not to follow his leadership. If she ever does relinquish temporary control to her husband, it is done in teeth-gritting obedience, rather than willing submission. The controlling woman's reluctant obedience is similar to the rebellious little girl who was required to sit down. The little girl sat, but she stubbornly maintained control as she said to herself, "I am sitting down on the outside, but I am standing up on the inside!"

Some indications of a self-righteous woman are incessant and insistent nagging, angry arguing (especially if someone does not appear to agree with her point of view), and penalizing anyone within her sphere of control who does not do what she thinks is best. Her punishments vary from cold-shoulder treatments and verbal abuse to pouting and crocodile tears. The self-important woman will use any form of intimidation or other manipulation to get her own way. In order to justify her actions she will often make favorable comparisons between herself and the supposed greater sins of someone else. A controlling woman is usually arrogant and smug. She is one of the most difficult women to live with because she is almost always argumentative, fault finding, and implacable (contentious and un-yielding.)

It is better to dwell in the wilderness, than with
a contentious and an angry woman
(Proverbs 21:19).

A continual dropping in a very rainy day and a
contentious woman are alike (Proverb 27:15).

Spiritual Superiority Thinking

One of the more insidious oppositions to Biblical womanhood comes from women who know the facts in the Bible very well. These women believe that their knowledge, and thus their presumed spirituality, somehow enables them to live by their own rules. For instance, faulty thinking might lead them to believe that it is not really necessary for them to follow the leadership of their spiritually "inferior" husbands.

All of God's Word becomes subject to the private interpretation of women who presume a spiritual superiority. They may even say that the Holy Spirit has revealed something different to them, thus allowing them to bypass the revealed Word of God. The Bible reveals that even the Holy Spirit receives His directions from God the Father. Therefore, a Biblical woman understands that He will never direct her to disobey God's Word or do anything that would not glorify Christ.

> *Howbeit when he, the Spirit of truth, is come,*
> *he will guide you into all truth: for he shall not*
> *speak of himself; but whatsoever he shall hear,*
> *that shall he speak: and he will shew you things*
> *to come. He shall glorify me: for he shall receive*
> *of mine, and shall shew it unto you*
> (John 16:13-14).

The woman who thinks that the Holy Spirit would give her insight that is in opposition to the Word is actually being deluded by her own human feelings or desire for spiritual autonomy. No one can claim to have true spiritual wisdom while living according to her own opinions and rejecting the Word of God.

> *But let him ask in faith, nothing wavering. For he that wavereth is like a wave of the sea driven with the wind and tossed. For let not that man think that he shall receive any thing of the Lord. A double minded man is unstable in all his ways* (James 1:5-8).

Note: The term "double minded" refers to a person who thinks schizophrenically – that is partially with the world's thinking, emotions, and personal opinions; and partially with God's Word. (See also, 2 Peter 1:20)

Oh, Wretched Woman That I Am!

This chapter has covered only four dominate sin-nature problems that can cause a woman to stray from Biblical womanhood. We have not considered other deeds of the flesh such as hatred, jealousy, and anger (Galatians 5:17-21) that also interferes with a woman's ability to live according to God's design. However, the discussion of these four problems should help you to realize that a major part of the opposition to God's design for women comes from a woman's own sin-nature. When a woman realizes the extensive influence that her own bent toward sin can have on her thinking, she may readily identify with Paul's emotion-filled statement concerning the struggle between his nature to sin and his desire to follow God's will.

> *But I see another law in my members, warring against the law of my mind, and bringing me into captivity to the law of sin which is in my members. O wretched man that I am! who shall deliver me from the body of this death?* (Romans 7:23-24).

All women struggle with one or more sin-nature problems that oppose Biblical womanhood. This fact makes it so easy to become discouraged – but, as always, God has provided the solution. Praise Him, for He has a plan that can destroy the effect of the opposition and give you victory over your human nature to sin. Without His provision we indeed would be left in our wretched state.

Defeating the Opposition

The ingrained opposition to God's design for our lives can be defeated by knowledge of, and adherence to, the Word of God. The Christian woman has available to her the means of resisting and overcoming the unbiblical influences in her life. She does not have to be swayed by false philosophies, nor is it necessary for her to succumb to her own sinful tendencies. The armament that defeats such opposition is spiritual thinking.

True spiritual thinking belongs to, and comes only from, God; it comes not from anything we feel, think, or can manufacture within ourselves. Only God's Word tells us how we can obtain *His* spirituality, both for eternal salvation and for living a godly life. When a woman accepts Jesus Christ as her personal Savior she is saved for eternity (John 3:36); she becomes a child of God (John 1:12); and she is able to have fellowship with Him in this life as well (1 John 1:9). While a woman is walking in fellowship with God, the Holy Spirit works to counter her sin nature weaknesses and produces in her the fruit of the Spirit. This is what is meant by true spirituality. The fruit of the Spirit utterly destroys any opposition to Biblical womanhood.

> *But the fruit of the Spirit is love, joy, peace, longsuffering, gentleness, goodness, faith, Meekness, temperance: against such there is no law* (Galatians 5:22-23).

The fruit of the Spirit in a believer's life manifests true spirituality, as compared to the false spirituality of the one claiming to follow a private interpretation of Scripture. The Holy Spirit produces in the believer only attitudes and actions that are in perfect harmony with God's laws. A woman cannot maintain true spirituality while she is living contrary to any of the written Word of God.

Therefore to him that knoweth to do good, and doeth it not, to him it is sin (James 4:17).

Living in opposition to God's Word is sin, and sin breaks spiritual communion between man and God. At that point, confession of sin is the only prayer that restores a believer's fellowship with God.

If we confess our sins, he is faithful and just to forgive us our sins, and to cleanse us from all unrighteousness. If we say that we have not sinned, we make him a liar, and his word is not in us (1 John 1:9-10). (cf Psalms 32:5; 51:1-9: Proverbs 28:13.)

An unshakeable confidence in Christ, knowledge of His Word, and walking daily in the Holy Spirit are the means by which a woman can resist the deceptive philosophies that work against the plan of God. Every thought that is brought to *the obedience of Christ* destroys the opposition and leads a woman to live to the glory of God.

Casting down imaginations, and every high thing that exalteth itself against the knowledge of God, and bringing into captivity every thought to the obedience of Christ; (2 Corinthians 10:5).

Living by a Truly Higher Spiritual Law

Under the law of our land, today's woman is free to make decisions in opposition to her husband's leadership. Among her legal rights, she is allowed to nullify his vote in elections, open credit accounts, divorce him without grounds, and make major life decisions without even consulting her husband. However, God calls believers to do what is right spiritually above what is "right" according to current governmental law, socially accepted tradition, or popular opinion. Following a higher spiritual law is the act of choosing what is right before God even though a human law grants you permission to do otherwise. The story of Philemon is a perfect example of a believer being asked to forgo his legal rights in favor of spiritual truth.

Philemon was a believer who was led to Christ by Paul. He had a slave named Onesimus who ran away and was therefore subject to death under the law of the land. After running away Onesimus met Paul and he too was won to Christ.

Paul wrote a letter to Philemon entreating him to deal with Onesimus by a higher spiritual law. In this letter Paul acknowledged that Philemon had every *legal right* to deal harshly with his errant servant. However, Paul appealed to God's higher spiritual laws of forgiveness and divine love in order to encourage Philemon to go beyond what he had a legal right to do.

> *I beseech thee for my son Onesimus, whom I have begotten in my bonds:* (Philemon 10)... *Having confidence in thy obedience I wrote unto thee, knowing that thou wilt also do more than I say* (Philemon 21).

The higher spiritual law surpasses mere compliance to laws. First, it is to know God's reason behind each law given to man, as David demonstrated:

> *For thou desirest not sacrifice; else would I give it: thou delightest not in burnt offering. The sacrifices of God are a broken spirit: a broken and a contrite heart, O God, thou wilt not despise* (Psalm 51:16-17).

Second, it is to act in Christian love and grace, *beyond* the letter of the law. It is to forgive *seventy times seven* (Matthew 18:22); not to divorce even though you have the right (Matthew 19:6-8); not to sue a fellow believer even though you have been wronged (I Corinthians 6:7); and for a woman to set aside her own rights in order to reach her husband for Christ (1 Peter 3:1 and 1 Corinthians 7:16).

This truly higher spiritual law does not mean that a believing woman will set aside God's written Word; it means that she *willingly* submits to every law of God and, even further, sacrifices her own rights for the benefit of others. If her husband does not live according to the Word of God, she does not use that as her excuse to forsake Biblical womanhood. In other words, she does not say to her mate, "I will be a Biblical wife *after* you act as a Biblical husband."

The Christian woman who consistently applies God's Word to her everyday life genuinely lives according to God's higher spiritual law. Even when her personal circumstances appear to warrant her justifiable retaliation, and everyone she knows encourages her that she has "the right," she still adheres to God's spiritual direction. Like the book of Philemon teaches, she goes beyond the letter of the law and does not demand her rights. A woman who lives according to this way of life offers love when her husband and children are unlovely, she gives when she has been rebuffed, and she does these things as a deliberate act of submission to God's will.

In Conclusion

It is not necessary for a Christian woman to fall as a casualty to vain philosophies or to succumb to her sin nature's resistance to Biblical womanhood. Christ has already destroyed such enemies. As believers we can claim our victory through him:

*But thanks be to God, which giveth us the victory
through our Lord Jesus Christ. Therefore, my
beloved brethren, be ye steadfast, unmoveable,
always abounding in the work of the Lord,
forasmuch as ye know that your labour is not in
vain in the Lord* (1 Corinthians 15:57-58).

Right now, today, you can simply obey the Word of God,
even if you do not feel like it. Remember, there is power in the
Word! Pray that God will change your mind through knowledge
of His Word and that He will change your emotions through
your obedience. Your trust in God will grow stronger as you
obey Him and as you watch Him work His miracles in your
life.

I pray that each of you will realize Christ's victory over
*every high thing that exalteth itself against the knowledge of
God* (1 Corinthians 10:5). As you steadfastly submit your will
to God's design for Biblical womanhood, I also pray that you
will have exceeding joy and full confidence that your *labor is
not in vain in the Lord* (1 Corinthians 15:58).

SECTION III

APPLICATIONS FOR
PRACTICAL LIVING

INTRODUCTION

If you have reached this section after carefully reading the first two sections, it indicates that you have a desire to live your life in obedience to God. On the other hand, if you have turned to this section out of curiosity, please go back and seriously study the first two sections before proceeding. The illustrations for practical living in this third section may sound like just opinions if you have not studied the Biblical substantiation on which they are based. It is the Word of God that should be the sustaining force in your life, not anyone's opinions. Once you have the Biblical foundation, you will be prepared to appreciate how Biblical womanhood truly applies to your life.

Applications for Practical Living, sets forth certain mechanics for living the principles taught in **Section I**. This section is Biblical womanhood and marriage placed into action. It gives specific how-to advice and should answer most of the questions brought to mind in **Section I**.

Applications ... should also provide encouragement and hope that you can actually live Biblical womanhood. However, you need to be aware that there are many powerful obstacles working against your success. Each woman is burdened with her own nature to sin. Although she may try to live as a Biblical wife she still struggles with her own desire for autonomy as well as outside forces that encourage her independence. In addition, she may struggle with the fear that her husband will misuse his leadership and cause her to suffer, or worse, cause her children to suffer. These struggles can cause a modern wife to feel very vulnerable. Furthermore, the actual imperfections of her spouse create possible stumbling blocks, as she must cope with problems that are not of her own making. Finally, she must overcome the modern vain philosophies that entreat her to doubt and fear God's perfect way for marriage.

Nevertheless, obstacles to Biblical womanhood can be overcome. Whether a modern Christian woman overcomes such barriers and lives as a Biblical wife depends entirely on her personal commitment to God. This commitment can inspire her to search for ways to accomplish God's goal of Biblical womanhood and give her the stamina to persevere, regardless of the barriers. This section will provide you with many practical illustrations on how to succeed as a Biblical woman in today's world.

CHAPTER XIV

DISILLUSIONS, DISAPPOINTMENTS, AND MISUNDERSTANDINGS

From the time a little girl is old enough to play house she often dreams of the day she will get married and "live happily ever after" like the princess in her favorite fairy tale. These dreams do not evaporate as a girl grows into a young woman. She continues to expect that she will someday marry a wonderful man and have a family of her own. A woman is at the height of her happiness on her wedding day because it signifies the beginning of the fulfillment of her life-long hopes and dreams. She has stardust in her eyes and her theme song is "I will love you forever." However, in no time at all the stardust begins to seem more like gritty fool's gold, and the theme song begins to sound more like, "Nobody knows the trouble I've seen." The fact is that a husband and wife can live together "happily ever after" only in fairy tales.

The unrealistic expectations of an immature girl toward marriage set her up for major disappointments. The reality of living with a human husband soon explodes the illusions that were promoted by those fairy tales. In real life, sin natures inevitably clash and the star-struck girl is forced to deal with disillusions, disappointments, and misunderstandings.

One source of disillusion for the Christian wife occurs when she knows how a Christian man is supposed to treat his wife; that is to love her *even as Christ also loved the church...* (Ephesians 5:25). A woman who understands what is perfect and right for a Biblical marriage may reasonably expect it to be that way. When it is not, she can feel cheated and disappointed. In order to deal with the realities of life she must not forget that although God's ways are perfect, the people who attempt to live His ways are decidedly imperfect.

A wife's disappointments in marriage can be because of her unrealistic expectations, or because even her reasonable expectations are not being met. In either case her disappointments will remain unresolved unless she faces her marriage realistically and Biblically. No wife can expect to have a trouble-free marriage. Marriage is a union of two imperfect people, one of whom is a husband who causes his wife some very real problems. The most practical first step to resolving problems with a husband is to understand the make-up of the man.

Understanding Your Husband

For a wife to live with her husband in a practical manner, she must make every effort to understand her man, as he actually is, not how she wants him to be. **Chapters VII, VIII**, and the following will help a woman to better understand the man who is her husband.

Many disappointments a wife faces in marriage are simply because of the differences between the drives of men and women. Most women are very relationship oriented. Courtship days are probably one of the most exciting times of a woman's life. During this time her future husband becomes the center of her life. She usually assumes that her fiancée wants to make her the center of his life as well. Therefore, when the wedding is over her and her husband's pursuit ceases somewhat, or even altogether, she may become confused and hurt. Because he no longer does the things he did while they courted, she may begin to feel that he does not love her anymore. A wife can overcome many of her disappointments when she accepts that her husband's drives in their relationship are not, nor ever will be, identical to her own.

In contrast to a woman's desire to make her man the center of her life, a man's major drive is to lead, protect, and provide for his family **(Chapter VII).** However, such responsibility is an extremely difficult, lonely, and challenging task. Therefore, a man's goal during courtship is to identify and to secure a supportive helpmate and companion – one who will provide him with a purpose to succeed. He feels a strong need for a wife to ease his loneliness and to support his responsibility. A man is often attracted to the woman who shares his dreams for the future and the one who encourages him during the times he feels like giving up.

Once a man has married, the objective of winning the woman of his choice is completed and the husband is now ready to move on to conquer his main pursuits – that of providing for a family. Furthermore, he expects his wife to move on to become his helpmate – that is to encourage him so that his task is less lonely and difficult. He too, may feel puzzled when he discovers that his wife wants to continue the activities of courtship, rather than move on to other objectives. This fact may not be very flattering to a woman's romantic, feminine soul; but men are motivated into action more by tangible goals than by their emotions.

It is not that a man is totally void of any emotional need for a close relationship with his wife, but it is not usually the major goal that he will aggressively work to achieve. Nevertheless, a husband who has a wife who will adjust her life to his can provide him with an intimate relationship that he cannot find anywhere else. A side benefit of a woman's willingness to adapt her life to her husband's is that she will also gain what she desires most – a close relationship with a beloved husband, who dearly loves and appreciates her. However, no matter how much a wife attempts to fit her life to her husband or how much she tries to understand his maleness, there will always be some problems between them that need to be solved.

Problem-Solving Through Communication

I cannot stress how important it is for a husband and wife to develop the art of mutual communication. Looking objectively at a problem and searching for principles that are in keeping with God's design for manhood and womanhood is the key to developing a close relationship in marriage. When a wife has some emotional needs that she desires for her husband to fill, she must be willing to communicate those needs in a manner that he can comprehend.

It can be a very emotional experience for a woman to talk with her husband about her needs. It must be remembered, however, that a woman will not properly communicate to an objective man when she is highly emotional. A man has a tendency to discount the importance of a woman's words when she is emotionally charged. For a woman to communicate with a man, she must speak in a language that penetrates his masculine way of thinking. The following basic steps will help prepare you for meaningful communication with your husband.

Preparation for Communication With a Man

Before you attempt to communicate with your husband about marriage problems, you need to prepare yourself mentally, emotionally, and spiritually.

1. *Examine and judge your own life.* Condemning another, even when they are wrong, does not make you right (Matthew 7:1-5; 2 Corinthians 10:12). The questions to ask of yourself are "Am I living my life according to the Biblical teaching for wives? Am I serving as a true helpmate, honoring my husband's leadership and supporting his manhood?"

2. *Be spiritually prepared.* Ask yourself, "Is God and His Word first in my life and am I walking closely with Him?" Make sure you are walking closely with God and, therefore, are able to approach your husband with a correct attitude.

3. *Pray* for God to prepare your husband's heart and to quiet your emotions so that you may have a constructive discussion.

After you have prepared *yourself* spiritually you are ready to approach your husband with your problem.

1. *Be considerate.* Choose your timing carefully. Do not try to talk to your husband when he is especially tired, worried, sick, or the minute he enters the door after work. Wait until he is relaxed and in a good mood.

2. *Prepare your husband for discussion.* For instance, you may ask him to set aside time to talk about a problem you are having. If he seems reluctant to talk at the exact moment that you have chosen, ask him to let you know when he will be able to talk with you. Be sure to tell him that your request is very important to you.

3. *Present your needs rather than accuse.* For instance, presenting needs could include, "I miss the talks we used to have. I really feel lonely and I need to be more a part of

your life." Accusations would include, "You never talk to me anymore. You shut me out of your life because you are insensitive."

Please, notice the objective, "I need" that comes across in the first example and the accusing "You bad boy" inference in the second. Your husband will most likely respond positively to a request, but he will definitely bristle and defend himself if he feels like a bad little boy who is in trouble with mommy.

1. *Help your husband fulfill your requests* by giving him suggestions that are goal-oriented. For instance, ask him if you could make it a practice to go out on a weekly date, or ask if he would turn off the TV for an hour each evening so you can talk about your days. Perhaps, you would like an evening walk, or _____ you fill in the blank with whatever would help provide the warmth that you need in your marriage. Again, this method gives your husband an objective goal he can accomplish, rather than confront him with a challenge that may make him feel attacked.

2. *Listen as well as talk.* The doors of communication go two ways, so be prepared to listen and be willing to make some personal changes. You may discover that when you talk to your husband about your unfulfilled needs, he has a complaint or two of his own. He may tell you that he does not talk to you because you do not give him time to unwind when he gets home from work. Your husband may reveal that you frequently interrupt him, or perhaps that you change the subject to your own interests and go on and on about details that are interesting only to you. There are many things that your husband may wish to tell you that will bring you closer together when you open the doors for two-way communication.

Giving Communication Time

After a woman has communicated a problem to her husband she usually expects some immediate changes to take place. However, this does not always occur. If your husband does slip back into his old ways and forgets the plan that you both agreed upon, it is all right to remind him. However, approach him in the same manner and with the same guidelines as before. Avoid resorting to techniques of nagging, belittling, shaming, or accusing him in order to get your own way; and *never* compare his actions with how other men treat their wives.

Habits are hard to change. Give your husband time to accomplish what you are asking of him. Also, pay close attention and show appreciation when he deliberately does what you wish, such as turning off the television to talk. Your appreciation will demonstrate that you are not trying to control his actions, but that your needs are real. If you do not notice his attempts to please you, or if you only point out when he errs, he will probably quit trying altogether.

When Things Do Not Improve

In every marriage a wife must accept that there are some things about her husband that will never change – at least not for a very long while. In such cases constant reminders tend only to sound like chronic complaining and usually avail nothing. A wife's attitude toward unchanging irritations should be an attitude of acceptance and forgiveness, just as the Lord has accepted and forgiven her.

> *Put on therefore, as the elect of God, holy and beloved, bowels of mercies, kindness, humbleness of mind, meekness, longsuffering; Forbearing one another, and forgiving one another, if any man have a quarrel against any:*

> *even as Christ forgave you, so also do ye. And*
> *above all these things put on charity, which is*
> *the bond of perfectness* (Colossians 3:12-14).

In the beginning of this chapter we spoke of fairy tales. In fairy tales the frog turns into a charming prince. In real life, the prince more often becomes a frog who gets mud on the carpet and embarrasses his princess in public. The truth is that living according to Biblical principles for womanhood means living with the frog, as well as the prince. Sometimes, putting Biblical principles into action means that a wife must deal with her less-than-charming husband while he acts immaturely, and she must continue to follow his leadership even while he is not walking rightly with God. Furthermore, she may suffer along side him during the unpleasant consequences of his immaturity and sin. A Biblical wife will honor her husband's position of authority, even if it takes fifty years for him to allow God to break that immaturity. Sometimes, I think that modern women would better comprehend the reality of their marriage vows if the wedding ceremony included:

> "I promise to trust God while my husband grows
> into maturity. I will learn to understand his
> masculine characteristics. I will remain
> respectful even when I think he is wrong. I will
> share the consequences of all his mistakes and I
> will persevere through all disillusions,
> disappointments, and misunderstandings, till
> death do us part."

As it is, most brides today believe that marriage is a 50/50 relationship and they promise to "love, honor, and obey," without the slightest hint of what they are getting into. The Biblical principle for marriage is not a 50/50 contractual arrangement. Instead, it is a 100% commitment on each individual's part. Granted, it is *easiest* when the other mate does his or her part. However, a believer is still responsible for giving his or her 100% commitment, even when their mate's sin nature is in full view. A Christian wife should operate within her role as a helpmate when her husband does or does not respond to her needs. In the end, it is not what another person does that commends us; but commendation comes to those who simply do what is right, without expectations of, or demands for, any immediate reward.

> *And let us not be weary in well doing: for in due season we shall reap, if we faint not. As we have therefore opportunity, let us do good unto all men, especially unto them who are of the household of faith* (Galatians 6:9-10).

CHAPTER XV

IRRITATIONS, FRUSTRATIONS, AND AGGRAVATIONS

If you have a typical marriage, your husband probably has at least one habit that drives you crazy. For instance, the bathroom is left like a gorilla just showered and shaved. He eats in a certain messy or disgusting manner; he puts his dirty socks on the coffee table, or _____ you fill in the blank. You and your husband will have a blend of your very own irritants.

A wife can nag her gorilla about how he leaves the bathroom, she can throw his socks at him, or as we saw in the last chapter she can learn to solve problems through objective communication. Communication is always the best way to deal with the problems that occur in a marriage. However, proper communication between husband and wife is sometimes difficult to achieve. Just as the different drives of men and women can pave the way for disappointments and misunderstandings, their different way of thinking can make communication extremely difficult. These differences cause miscommunication, which can be a major hindrance to the resolution of problems in marriage.

Let us look at three examples of how poor communication can separate a husband and a wife and how it can prevent them from resolving their problems. Following each example we will see how a wife can simultaneously use objective communication principles, find a solution to her problem, and be a Biblical helpmate to her husband.

Example One: What is Wrong With This Picture?

John has a habit of returning home from work each evening and immediately sitting down to read his newspaper – barely remembering to even say, "Hi." Mary is tired of this routine and on this particular evening she glares at the back of the newspaper, sighs, and goes into the kitchen slamming the door behind her. After about ten minutes, John becomes aware that there is a lot of noise going on in the kitchen. He can hear Mary muttering as she roughly tosses pots and pans onto the stove and slams the refrigerator door. John calls out, "What is wrong with you?" to which Mary replies, "If you loved me, you would know what is wrong!"

What is wrong with this picture is that Mary is holding John responsible for understanding something that he is not built to understand. John may love his wife very much, but love alone does not help him decode Mary's words and angry actions. In this case it is up to Mary to communicate objectively to John what her problem is and how he can help her solve it.

Let Us Correct This Picture

Mary should evaluate what it is that is making her feel frustrated and angry. For instance, her thoughts may be, "John never talks to me anymore." Next, she should present her need to John. This part is tricky. Remember, a woman's thoughts are never far removed from her emotions, but her emotions do not communicate well to a man's "just the facts" way of thinking. For instance, "John **never** talks to me anymore," is a statement from Mary's emotional reaction to the **feeling** of being shut out, rather than a clear declaration of what is actually true. If Mary presents only her feelings to John, she will communicate something entirely different than what she means to say. John would most likely take her emotional words literally and his first reaction would be, "That is ridiculous, of course I talk to you. I asked you what was wrong, and I am talking to you *now* aren't I?"

In order to convey her thoughts properly, Mary needs to translate her feelings into the factual words that will accurately acquaint John with her real need – in this case, conversation. The translation from female language (a expressive language of feelings) to male language (a literal language) is necessary before John can provide what Mary truly needs. To gain what she desires without instigating an argument, Mary might say, "John after you have rested for a while, I need to talk to you." Then, when John is ready to talk, Mary could say, "Lately, I have been feeling lonely. I have evaluated why I am feeling this way (he will love to hear you have analyzed your feelings) and I realized it is because we are not talking like we once did. I really need for us to set aside time each evening for conversation."

God's Word instructs a husband to provide for his wife's needs in a loving and understanding way. Most husband's would be quite happy to provide what their wives need – **if** they could just understand what that is. A wife is functioning as a Biblical helpmate when she helps her husband understand how to fulfill his role as a loving husband. In most cases, all a wife must do is to respect her husband's objectivity and translate her feelings into concrete goals that he can both understand and successfully accomplish. If a woman is willing to learn this translation technique, she will be in a better position to achieve the closeness that both she and her husband will enjoy.

Example Two: The Case of The Unconscious Husband

There are many irritations and aggravations that can occur simply because a woman has standards for housekeeping to which her husband is oblivious. For instance, I know one woman whose husband would invariably wash his hands in the kitchen just after she left a colander of lettuce draining in the sink. It drove her crazy when he absentmindedly rinsed the soap from his hands right on top of the lettuce. This wife repeatedly complained to her husband, but to no avail. Finally, she realized that part of the problem was that her husband was not aware of the lettuce in the sink at all. When she said, "Do not wash your hands there!" she did not fully communicate. Since she never mentioned the lettuce, her literal husband thought that his wife objected to him *ever* washing his hands in the kitchen. He considered his wife's complaints totally unreasonable.

Finally, the woman in our illustration realized that the way she worded her problem caused her husband to feel under personal attack. Her solution was to make her complaint impersonal by drawing her husband's attention to the inanimate lettuce. She began to say, "Honey, let me remove the lettuce before you wash your hands." It only took a few repetitions before her husband became aware of the real problem, and now he removes the lettuce from the sink without reminders. This approach not only eliminates a great deal of irritation, it also saves a lot of lettuce.

Example Three: The Unsolvable Problem

There are some annoying habits that a husband will never change. For instance, the husband in our above illustration has a habit of shaking his freshly washed hands before drying them. Now, when this man does something he does it with vigor, so water is splattered everywhere when he shakes his hands (a little like a wet dog). No matter how his wife has worded her problem, this husband's habit went unchanged for more than thirty years.

When a woman must live with small irritations that never seem to change, they can begin to grow in her mind until they become mountainous frustrations. The wife in our illustration realized that her frustration level was growing far out of proportion to the seriousness of the offense. This wife knew that the only solution was to change her own attitude, rather than expect her husband to change his habit. First, she reminded herself that when her husband goes on trips, her dry counter tops and mirrors become lonely reminders that he is away. When he is gone for a very long time, she misses his presence so much that she would gladly clean up water spots just to have him home again. Why not maintain that same positive attitude when he is not away but is at home splattering mirrors? After all, how important is a little water compared to the love, provision, protection, honor, and companionship that he so freely gives to her? By modifying her own attitude, this wife now smiles while she cleans mirrors and counter tops. She can even laugh about and enjoy her husband's eccentricities. Sometimes a simple decision to look at problems in a more positive manner can eliminate frustration and elicit appreciation instead.

A wife is to be her husband's helper on earth, which includes helping him to be aware of her needs. But it is not her job as a helpmate to force changes. A wife's love and acceptance may eventually produce in her husband a desire to make positive changes, but angry demands will seriously damage their relationship. However, there is hope. An interesting phenomenon often occurs when a wife accepts her husband as he is – he may begin to change some of his habits on his own. It is as if the husband is tuning out what sounds to him like nagging, but once he feels fully accepted by his wife he may make a special effort to please her. This happened for me. After years of complaining about soap on my lettuce, my husband cooperated within two days – after I changed *my* attitude. And, after more than thirty years of marriage, my husband is now drying the counter tops and mirrors after he washes and shaves. Changing your own attitude can produce miraculous rewards in time. More importantly, a Biblical woman's patient spirit is better than a prideful, demanding one, and a loving spirit is more pleasing than an angry spirit in God's eyes.

> *Better is the end of a thing than the beginning thereof: and the patient in spirit is better than the proud in spirit. Be not hasty in thy spirit to be angry: for anger resteth in the bosom of fools* (Ecclesiastes 7:8-9).

CHAPTER XVI

SUPPORTING YOUR HUSBAND'S LEADERSHIP ROLE

God established the man's leadership responsibility; sinful men did not create it because they had a lust for power. The husband's role can be traced back to God's design for mankind, long before sin tainted Adam's and Eve's actions (1 Corinthians 11:3 & 7-9; Ephesians 5:31 compared with Genesis 2:24 and 1 Timothy 2:12-14).

Although sin diminished Adam's ability to lead perfectly, his accountability to God for leading Eve remained in tact. The first indication after the fall that sin had not shifted this responsibility is illustrated in Genesis 3:9 when God asked Adam, *Where art thou?* Eve had sinned first, but God did not seek her out first. He called to Adam because the man was in the leadership position. Adam's sin was twofold. Not only did he choose to eat of the forbidden fruit, but also he followed Eve's leadership rather than fulfill his own responsibility of leadership (Genesis 3:17a).

Throughout the Old Testament, husbands were clearly accountable to God for the leadership of their families. The accounts of Noah, Abraham, Isaac, Jacob, and others illustrate this well. The Bible tells of many events where sin corrupted these husbands' leadership, but that did not change their God-appointed roles. Today, husbands continue to be responsible for the leadership of their wives as evidenced by the verses already referenced above, as well as 1 Timothy 3:4-5.

Some believe that Adam chose to eat the forbidden fruit because he did not want to lose Eve. Whether this is true or not, we do not know for sure. What we do know is that for some reason Adam did choose to follow Eve's direction and to disobey God. From that day forward men have continued to fall into the same sin as Adam. Christian men today often fear their wives' reaction to their leadership more than they fear disobeying God. They choose to do what is safe and expedient, rather than what is correct, and their families suffer because of their failure. It is of great importance that a Biblical wife does not give her husband cause to fear that she will reject his leadership decisions.

Numerous Christian women intellectually accept the Biblical evidence that their husbands are responsible for leadership, but they still have a problem putting that knowledge into practice. Sin corrupts a woman's willingness to follow, just as it corrupts a man's proficiency in leading. This chapter will discuss some of the skills a wife needs in order to obey God and follow her all-too-human husband. We will deal with three types of real-life husbands that a wife could conceivably have. The first example deals with a husband who has little desire to lead his family at all. This is the passive husband; or the man who is not a natural leader. The second example discusses the husband who may be a natural leader, but is over-bearing in his practice. He will be called the aggressive husband. The third example concerns a Christian woman's fear of following an unspiritual husband. The unspiritual man can either be an unbeliever or a believer who is not committed at this time in his personal relationship with God.

As you read this chapter keep in mind that few men are always passive, always aggressive, or always out of touch with God. A husband's leadership will vary somewhere between these three extremes. His leadership may fluctuate from time to time and from issue to issue. For instance, a husband may be an excellent father, but exercise domineering control over his wife's life as if she were a child. Or, he may be a great provider, but be completely indifferent to his role as spiritual leader of his family. Each husband is a unique mixture of his own sin nature traits, his background, and his personal development. It is not possible to cover the many specific problems that a wife might face in her marriage. However, the three problem areas mentioned above are discussed along with solutions on how a wife can be an effective helpmate, even under husbands with the most extreme types of personality. You will then need to discern which principles are to be utilized with your husband. You will discover that the information presented can normally be mixed and matched to your particular type of man.

Type One: The Passive Husband

A large portion of our male population today tends toward being passive. This has partly been the result of incorrect child training; of which we have had an abundance of in the past few generations. The passive male may also have had painful experiences that severely damaged his masculinity that will tend to make him insecure about his leadership abilities.

At this time in American history there are an especially large number of passive, or effeminate, men in our churches. These men are fearful of the accountability that is inherent in leadership and they tend to be more affected by their emotions than guided by their intellect and masculinity. They will typically procrastinate in making decisions, hoping time will make it unnecessary, or that someone else will relieve them of the responsibility. As a result, more and more women have taken over the leadership positions in Sunday schools and church activities.

At home, passive men prefer to share leadership responsibilities with their wives. Sometimes, women choose to marry passive men because they appear to be less demanding and more easily managed. Once married, however, these women become frustrated and resentful because they feel they must make all the decisions for the family. (These statements are not meant to attack men, nor are they meant to provide excuses for the women who have assumed control. They are simply my sad observations about the demise of male leadership and the rise of female controls throughout the Christian community.)

Regrettably, the woman who usurps her husband's position of leadership only encourages his deficiencies and provides him with an excuse to avoid his responsibility. For instance, a wife who is concerned about her husband's poor decisions concerning money only makes it easier for him to remain irresponsible when she insists on controlling the family budget. While she is trying to prevent short-ranged problems (like a poor credit record) her financially irresponsible husband is being prevented from facing the consequences for his actions. If he had to deal with the consequences of his over-spending, he might in time learn from the experience. However, his wife's controlling tactics abort this learning experience, and therefore, he will probably continue his wasteful habits (sometimes on the sly to keep "mommy" from knowing.)

In spite of the family difficulties caused by a passive man, an understanding Biblical wife can nurse her husband's ailing ego and encourage him to overcome his insecurities. A Biblical helpmate will encourage her husband in his proper masculine role without mothering him, teaching him, or taking over his responsibilities before God. The following guidelines of what a Biblical wife *can* do will help clarify how to be the best helpmate to a passive husband.

1. Pray fervently that God will cause your husband to become alert to his leadership responsibilities. Pray for your own strength to endure with grace the consequences that may occur in the family because of his lack of leadership.

2. Do not criticize. Constant criticism demolishes a man's ego and informs your husband that he does not measure up to your standards for manhood. This only results in making a passive man weaker.

3. Respectfully ask for your husband's leadership and insight, *even on decisions you could make yourself.* Then, do things his way. If he wants you to pay the bills because he hates the details of the job, do so, but ask him to set the budget.

Be sure to tell your husband how much you appreciate his insight whenever he gives you good advice. However, should his advice fail, do not be overly distressed by the failure; simply ask him how to fix the problem. Never say, "I told you so" when things go wrong. Fear of your reaction to his mistakes can only tempt your husband to withdraw his future leadership.

4. Most passive husbands are hesitant to take a firm stand on anything. They also do not usually respond quickly to requests for advice. Therefore, present your need for a leadership decision, and then offer to wait for his thoughts.

Patiently leave the decision in his hands. It is a wife's responsibility to let her husband know the date that a decision must be made and the cost for missing that date – **once**. Yes, watch things go undone, if necessary. If he later asks why something has gone undone, simply explain you are waiting for his decision on the matter. Remember, the take-over-wife may solve today's problem with repetitive reminders, but she also promotes her husband's inactive leadership. Furthermore, her shortsighted impatience may assure hundreds of future problems.

5. If your husband specifically asks you to do something, do it immediately. When a passive husband asks for something, even if it is just a timid hint, that *is* his leadership. Do not insist that he issues a direct order before you will act on what you already know he wants you to do. Be ready to please and willing to follow even his indirect attempts at leadership.

6. It is imperative for a passive husband to have a wife who does not debate or critique his every decision. Treating his timid decisions as if he might be making some terrible mistake will only defeat your goal of encouraging his leadership. If you must ask questions about his decision in order to clarify what is expected of you, do so with a respectful attitude and make sure he knows you are willing to follow.

7. Be mindful that it takes time for anyone to make positive changes in their life. A passive husband needs for his wife to accept him as he is *before* he will be motivated to improve. This can take a long while. In the meantime, "minor" in his shortcomings and "major" in his positive character traits.
8. Make a list of all your husband's qualities and then

practice showing him appreciation in those areas. There is no better medicine for encouraging a passive husband than honest praise for who and what he is already.

I am not suggesting that a wife should ever use dishonest flattery or manipulative techniques. The goal behind honest praise is for the benefit of another, but the goal of flattery is to get something for self. Biblical praise and appreciation encourages a man for his accomplishments, while manipulative techniques promote weakness. The following is an illustration of how a woman's schemes of self-interest promote weakness in the man who succumbs to her manipulation.

A certain wife did not like her husband's relatives and wanted to spend every holiday exclusively with her own family. After several years of neglecting his family, the husband began to feel guilty. However, every time he tried to discuss the issue with his wife she would say, "Let's discuss that later," and she would then ply her husband with excessive flattery. Her husband subconsciously understood this wife's manipulative technique, and he was aware that he was exchanging his leadership role for deceitful praise, but he acquiesced anyway. As a result he saw himself as a weak man who could be easily controlled by the flesh, and he disrespected his wife for using his weakness for her own purposes.

By contrast, a Biblical wife's honest words of praise will not result in weakening her husband's opinion of her or of himself.

Type Two: The Aggressive Husband

The aggressive husband can be described as opinionated, demanding, and domineering. Believe it or not, this man is just as insecure as is the passive one. In order to cover up feelings of inadequacy the passive man retreats while the aggressive man attacks. Both men have egos that have been damaged or untrained, and both need the help and understanding acceptance of their wives. Therefore, a Biblical wife should treat her aggressive husband with the same tender care she would extend to a passive husband. Honest praise and appreciation for his talents is just as important for the aggressive husband as it is for the passive one. In addition, a wife can take the following steps in order to help her husband realize that intimidation is not necessary to cause her to follow his lead.

1. Pray that God will cause your husband to become aware of the need for consideration for how others may feel. Pray for your own strength and spiritual wisdom in dealing with your husband.

2. Trust God for emotional protection for both you and your children.
> *Cast thy burden upon the LORD, and he shall sustain thee: he shall never suffer the righteous to be moved* (Psalm 55:23).

3. Treat your husband with all the understanding, kindness, and forgiveness that you possible can give.
> *Put on therefore, as the elect of God, holy and beloved, bowels of mercies, kindness, humbleness of mind, meekness, longsuffering; Forbearing one another, and forgiving one*

another, if any man have a quarrel against any:
even as Christ forgave you, so also do ye
(Colossians 3:12-13).

4. Be willingly submissive. Never speak to your husband in an attacking manner and never retaliate with attacks on his manhood. A soft reply defuses unfair or angry demands much faster than does retaliation or a refusal to comply.
   A soft answer turneth away wrath: but grievous
   words stir up anger (Proverbs 15:1).

5. Most likely you are not the reason your husband has developed an intimidating personality, but be prepared to consider that your actions might compound a problem that already exists. Have you been argumentative, debated his every decision, rejected his leadership, or been unappreciative of what he has done well? Have you challenged his manhood in some way? (Review: **Chapters V through IX.**) Be willing to make changes in yourself if necessary.

6. Very often a man's aggressiveness is an act of self-protection. Such a man is usually unable to trust that other people do not intend to cause him emotional harm. Therefore, it is important that a wife earn her husband's trust by showing him that his best interest is the reason for all that she says or does. A wife, who gets in the habit of verbal attacks, snide remarks, or cutting put-downs, will never gain her husband's trust. Difficult as it is to pet a porcupine, you can get one to roll over and allow you to stroke its stomach after you have gained its trust. Although it is very difficult to hold your tongue while another person is verbally attacking you, it can be done. If a wife wishes to help her aggressive husband she must refrain from becoming aggressive herself.

> *He that is slow to wrath is of great*
> *understanding: but he that is hasty of spirit*
> *exalteth folly* (Proverbs 14:29).

7. Important! Calmly tell your husband that his harsh words and actions hurt you. Help him understand that you want to be his helpmate and that a more gentle request is all that is necessary. Before you talk to him, however, be sure your attitude is not defensive or attacking. Do not condemn him, but do let him know how much his aggression hurts you. Also, before you do this be sure you are actually willing to comply with his requests.

Type Three: The Unspiritual Husband

There are two types of unspiritual husbands – the one who is unsaved, and the one who is saved but is not committed to living the Christian way of life. A Christian wife should treat her unspiritual husband with the same respectful and submissive attitude she would do for the most spiritual husband, plus:

1. Pray for God to reveal to your husband his need for salvation or commitment to live for God. Do not badger him, constantly tell him he is a sinner, or infer that you think of him as an inferior.

2. Teach your children to respect and obey their father. Do not undermine his authority by implying in any way that there is something wrong with their father. In fact, it is best if they do not know his spiritual condition, at least not until they are old enough to handle the knowledge without feelings of judgment or superiority. The admonition of 1 Peter 3 is the same for wives of unbelieving husbands as it is for wives of uncommitted Christian husbands.

*Likewise, ye wives, be in subjection to your own
husbands; that, if any obey not the word, they
also may without the word be won by the
conversation of the wives; While they behold
your chaste conversation coupled with fear*
(1 Peter 3:1-2).

3. Put yourself in God's hands and be prepared for pressure
to come to bear in your husband's life. When you pray for
God to reveal to your husband his need for salvation (or for
his need for a committed Christian life) God will be working
to capture your husband's attention. Pressures may come
to bear that are intended by God to cause your husband to
be receptive to His Word. (Loss of job, illness, or accidents,
has been used in the past to bring tough guys to their knees.)
This time period will be critical for both you and your
husband. A loving and supportive Biblical wife is perhaps
even more important at this time than at any other. You
must be willing to endure the pressures that God intends to
use as a means to turn your husband to Him. You must
endure while you also refrain from attempting to remove
those pressures. If you try to protect your husband from
experiencing difficulties in his life, you will be interfering
with God's purposes for those pressures. However, if you
persist in being a Biblical wife, your loyalty can be the basis
of a deeper relationship with your husband. God may even
use your example to draw your husband to Himself.

*But let it be the hidden man of the heart, in that
which is not corruptible, even the ornament of
a meek and quiet spirit, which is in the sight of
God of great price. For after this manner in the
old time the holy women also, who trusted in
God, adorned themselves, being in subjection
unto their own husbands:* (1 Peter 3:4-5).

4. Be diligent about your own spiritual life. Study the Word of God and apply the principles within it. Go to a church where you will be saturated with the teaching of God's Word. However, here comes the tough part: some husbands may be adamantly against attending church on Sundays. If your husband demands that you do not go to church, it is recommend that you do not go – at least for a while. If he only knows one verse of the Bible, it will be the one about wives submitting to their husbands.

There are many ways to receive Bible teaching and Christian fellowship with other women in the interim without going to Sunday services. Midweek, daytime classes, books, personal Bible reading, tapes, and the friendship of other believing women can carry you for a while. Yes, church is the optimum place to learn the Word, have fellowship, and exercise your spiritual gift, but first things first. God wants you in a Bible teaching church even more than you want it. Give Him a chance to arrange it His way, while perhaps winning your husband at the same time.

My husband was once on a radio talk show and mentioned this same concept of submitting to a husband, even by not attending church if necessary. Two ladies called the show and testified that God answered their prayers in exactly this manner. One woman said that she was at first fearful that she would never be able to go to church, but she decided to pray, be a Biblical wife, and trust God. Within a year her husband was so impressed with her submissive attitude that he not only allowed her to attend church but he went with her. Her husband was "won" by the behavior of his 1 Peter 3 wife when he later accepted Christ as his Savior.

I believe that most husbands will not prevent their submissive wives from attending church, at least not for very long. Those husbands who do so are usually the ones whose wives use their religion like a battering ram. Such a wife wields the Bible like a knife intended to condemn her husband, and yet, rarely adheres to Biblical principles herself by being the gentle spirit God calls her to be. Her husband invariably believes that the church condones his wife's defiant words and actions, and therefore, he wants nothing to do with Christianity. Non-submissive, religious harassment will seriously limit the possibility of a wife being God's instrument to win her husband to Christ. Her lack of grace will usually just prolong her own agony and her husband's as well.

In Conclusion

Just as most women today do not begin marriage as mature helpmates, few men enter marriage as accomplished leaders. Furthermore, every husband has at least one area of life where he lacks maturity. A Biblical wife must develop a long-ranged viewpoint toward her husband. She should seek solutions to problems that will be beneficial to them both even if it takes a long time to achieve favorable results. She must avoid temporary solutions that provide her with only temporary relief, but creates barriers for the future.

A Biblical wife should not think she must fix all problems her husband might have. Her husband's shortcomings are in capable hands when they are left for God to deal with in His own timeframe. A wife can pray about any problems she may see in her husband's life, but she must understand that she is not her husband's conscience, his new mother, or his spiritual leader. She can discuss and make suggestions, but she should not attempt to protect him from the natural consequences of his own immaturity. A wife can help with the implementation of a plan, but it is not her mission to remove her husband's responsibility of leadership by controlling all the details of the plan. A woman is responsible, however, to tend to her own areas of immaturity and to allow God to develop the Biblical characteristics that will enable her to be an effective Christian and helpmate. Sometimes, God even uses an imperfect husband as the means to develop a woman's maturity and Biblical virtues.

Perhaps the most important virtue any wife can possess is a loving attitude that radiates a willingness to sacrifice her personal interests for her husband's benefit. A gentle attitude will help her to speak honestly, but kindly, even while discussing delicate subjects. It will cause her to look for ways to encourage her husband, and it will cause her to refrain from ever treating him callously because of his shortcomings. A loving attitude will prevent a wife from retaliating when telling her husband that what he has said or done has hurt her. It will cause her to be diligent in her own spiritual life, to pray fervently for all those whom she loves, and to depend entirely on the grace of God for the final outcome.

Biblical truth will get a wife through any circumstance that can occur with a real-life husband, simply because her hope is rooted in her omnipotent God. God's omnipotence (all power) parted the sea for Moses and His power is able to steer any passive, aggressive, disobedient, or unbelieving husband in whatever direction He so deems necessary. How God chooses to move an errant husband, however, is rarely as dramatic as the parting of the sea. More often, He uses a Biblical wife who remains submissive and empathetic, even when her husband is not all he should be. A Biblical wife can believe God's Word, just as Moses did. When she possesses Biblical characteristics and faithfully acts upon God's principles for womanhood, she will be walking dry-shod across her own sea of testing and glorifying Him with each step.

CHAPTER XVII

SUPPORTING YOUR HUSBAND'S ROLE AS PROVIDER AND PROTECTOR

When a business leader has the help of a competent and cooperative staff, he is able to increase his effectiveness many times over. In the same way the quality of a helpmate's influence makes a positive impact on her husband's success as leader, provider, and protector. In the preceding chapters, we discovered the impact of a wife's influence on her husband's leadership. This chapter will discuss how a wife can encourage her husband's responsibility as provider and protector.

The Biblical Model

From the very beginning of time God made it clear that men were to protect and provide for their wives. Men were to till the soil, to be drafted and fight the wars, and to take care of their own families. In fact, in the New Testament a man who provided *not for his own, and specially for those of his own house, he hath denied the faith, and is worse than an infidel* (1 Timothy 5:8).

A husband's responsibilities as provider and protector are also derived from Scripture references that portray God as a husband to believers. In Deuteronomy 10:18 God speaks of Himself as a husband to Israel who executes justice (protection) for the fatherless and widow and who gives the stranger nourishment (provision). The New Testament refers to Christ as the husband of the church in 2 Corinthians 11:2 and Revelation 21:2 & 9. The model for how a human husband is to lead, provide, and protect is Christ.

> *For the husband is the head of the wife, even as Christ is the head of the church: and he is the saviour of the body... Husbands, love your wives, even as Christ also loved the church, and gave himself for it;* (Ephesians 5:23 & 25).

A husband's responsibility for protecting and providing for a wife and family gives balance to his leadership authority. A man may be the master of his castle, but his sense of protectiveness tempers the power of his authority. For this reason, it is a woman's distinct advantage to support and encourage her husband's masculinity in the areas of provision and protection.

Supporting Your Husband's Role as Provider

Inherent within a man is the awareness that he alone bears the ultimate responsibility to support his wife and family – even if his wife also works. Because even very masculine or well-trained men are secretly anxious that they will not be able to live up to this responsibility of manhood, they are very vulnerable to feelings of failure if their wives do not appreciate their efforts. When a wife appreciates her husband's provisional efforts she helps bolster his manly confidence. Her support comforts him while he works under difficult bosses, gives him courage when he faces competitive fellow employees, and eases the fatigue of long hours at a job he may even dislike. The following are some specific ways a helpmate can encourage her husband in his effort to provide for his family.

1. ***Do*** help make his home a retreat from the rigors of the workplace. Ask your husband how you can make your home special for him. He may want a special chair that no one else uses, or perhaps a special spot to spread out his hobby. No matter how large, or how small your home is, make it a place where he can rest and recover from the hardships of his workplace. A home can be a husband's castle as well as his wife's nest to feather.

2. ***Do*** find out what your husband needs in order to unwind after work. I once knew a husband who asked his wife for a glass of iced tea and thirty quiet minutes with the paper before dinner. This request unbelievably became a major contention between the couple. The wife thought that her days were too busy with the children for her to remember to have tea ready when he arrived home. She complained that the children were too hungry to wait for dinner and that he was thinking only of himself; therefore, she dismissed his simple request as selfish and unreasonable. This husband interpreted his wife's attitude to mean that she considered his needs trivial and bothersome. Tragically, he later sought out another woman who appeared more sensitive to his needs.

I am *not* suggesting that this marriage ended just because the husband did not get his glass of iced tea. The wife's resistance to preparing tea was merely an overt symptom of her underlying poor attitude toward her husband. Her negative attitude permeated everything she did and said. Nor am I excusing the husband for his adultery. He was as deficient a leader as she was a helpmate. I am only pointing out the significant role that this wife played in the break-up of her own marriage.

3. ***Do*** sympathetically listen to your husband's work difficulties and be a sounding board as he talks about possible solutions for his problems. *Beware*, however, that a husband does not need for his wife to take over and try to solve all his dilemmas. A Biblical helpmate encourages her husband to persevere *through* his troubles; a take-over wife tries to help him escape *from* his responsibilities. Usually, all a husband needs is a sympathetic listener and a helpmate to stand by him in his final decision. In this way she is encouraging him to fulfill his responsibility as provider.

4. ***Do*** carefully manage the household within your husband's income. The money a husband receives for his labor represents the sacrifice of many hours of his personal life; it is, therefore, a portion of himself. A wife's proper handling of her husband's money is proportional to the respect she has for him personally and for his life-sacrifice.

A wife needs to be very careful about how she treats her husband's provision. Even seemingly innocent remarks, such as apologizing to visitors for the cheapness of their furniture, can cause a husband to feel like a failure as a provider. A wife, who constantly complains that her husband does not earn enough, or squanders what he does provide, may suppress her husband's effectiveness at work. Furthermore, if she frequently demands extra luxuries that are beyond his ability to give she tells him that he is deficient as a provider.

On the other hand, a wife who becomes an expert at money-management helps her husband provide for his family successfully – no matter what his income may be. Her loving care for their possessions and her appreciation for his provision may bolster his ambition and encourage him to be more effective at his job.

Supporting Your Husband's Role as Protector

For thousands of years men have stood guard against attackers and even given their lives in order to protect their families. It is not difficult to recognize a wife's need for her husband's protection in dangerous situations, but often a wife misses the more subtle things that her husband may do out of his sense of protectiveness.

The following are some of the ways a husband today might supply his wife with safety and security:

1. He makes sure the car is in safe working order.

2. He will try to buy or rent a home in a decent neighborhood.

3. He keeps the home in safe repair with strong locks on the doors.

4. He provides insurance and/or investment funds for his family's future.

5. He is there when his wife cries "help."

6. He tries to shield his wife from evil influences that might harm her physically, emotionally, or spiritually. Protectiveness is why a husband sometimes objects when his wife watches certain television programs, reads books that are Biblically incorrect, or even when she spends too much time with certain worldly friends. A husband may be alert that such "entertainment" could negatively influence his wife's spiritual life.

7. He asks his wife not to get involved in, or at least to limit, certain activities (even worthwhile ones) because he knows her tendency to over-extend her energies. (This could include politics, community work, committees, and even some church events.)

8. He chooses a church where the Word of God is faithfully taught and where he believes his family is protected from false teaching.

All of the above are expressions of a husband's protectiveness toward his wife and family. When he offers his hand as his wife steps off a curb, or when he opens a door for her, a husband is expressing the protective side of his manhood. Sadly, many women in our modern society are rejecting such expressions of male protection. As a result men have begun to withdraw even greater forms of protection. This has made women increasingly vulnerable to harm.

In 1914, when the Titanic sank, approximately 75% of the women were saved while only 20% of the men survived. However, by 1992 when a survey called the "Titanic Test" was taken among 200 adults, protectiveness toward women had decreased dramatically. It was found that: If the Titanic sank today, only 67% of the men would be willing to give up their lifeboat seats for their spouses and a little more than 33% of the men would give their seats to a woman other than their wives.

In 1987 a ferry sank in the Philippines killing over 4000 people – mostly women and children. The majority of the survivors were men. When the male survivors were questioned why they had not helped the women and children, they were quoted as saying: "Hey, its survival of the fittest. It was every man for himself. If women want equality so much – they've got it!"

I believe one of the reasons men are less protective of women today than in 1914 is because modern women reject even the simplest gestures of men's protectiveness. Many women desperate to prove they do not need men show disdain when a man even opens a door for them. As women have forced their way into dangerous occupations that were once traditionally dominated by males, men began to lose their desire to protect. Women now serve in such hazardous positions as police and fire "persons," as well as on the front lines of military combat. Women have been very instrumental in desensitizing men's thoughts about the vulnerability of women. Today, countless men (happily, not all – yet) will just stand and watch as an elderly or a pregnant woman struggles to lift and carry a heavy load. I have even experienced (more than once) opening a heavy door at a store while a young male rushed in ahead of me. In effect, this senior citizen opened the door for a strong male forty years her junior.

A wife can be an effective helpmate or an influence for her own destruction. If she discourages her husband from functioning as the leader, provider, and protector of his family, the effect will be devastatingly destructive to his manhood and consequently to her security. When a husband's manhood is damaged he can become a weak, effeminate male whose inability to protect his wife shames him in his own eyes, as well as in hers. Or, he can become an insensitive brute who is always trying to prove his superiority physically. On the other hand, a husband whose efforts are appreciated by his wife can develop a healthy masculine picture of himself as a "real man." The leadership, provision, and protectiveness of a "real man" can enrich a woman's entire life and greatly increase her sense of security.

CHAPTER XVIII

WOMEN WORKING OUTSIDE OF THE HOME

Throughout human history most people have had to labor long hours daily just to survive. Today, however, factories, department stores, and grocery stores provide most of a family's physical needs. For instance, meat is butchered and cleanly packaged for us; staples come in boxes, bottles, and cans; and most produce is picked in the grocery store rather than reaped from a garden.

Where we once labored to produce the items we needed for survival, we now work for the money to purchase those products. In addition, we work so we will be able to acquire possessions and services that go far beyond our basic survival needs. Once called luxuries – automobiles, large homes, appliances, and closets full of clothing off-the-rack – are all items that modern Americans now consider absolute necessities. Not only do we call these products necessary but we also desire to own bigger, better, and more of every new item in the marketplace.

Many of the products available in our modern society have definitely eased our lives and we would not want to give them up. However, they have also changed our purpose for working and altered our thinking about what is beneficial to our families. Costly prepared mixes and entire microwave meals have contributed to the demise of creative cooking. The superiority of homegrown and made-from-scratch meals has been exchanged for lesser quality and speedy preparation. In addition, we prefer to pay others to do the jobs we no longer have the time, or the desire, to do ourselves – such as teaching and training our own children.

Furthermore, we have even changed the manner in which we help others. Most Americans prefer to use money as a means to render aid to those in need rather than to become involved on a more personal level. They expect their taxes to pay someone else to educate children and supply health care for the sick, elderly, and impoverished. And, they insist that government provides aid to people who have experienced catastrophic losses in their lives.

In just a few generations, American's purpose for working has drastically changed from the necessity for survival to the drive for money and things. Our perceived need for things has long surpassed the earning capacity of most husbands. Many would argue that the two-income family is a modern necessity. But, is it truly a necessity or a choice? Is it time to discern between that which we truly need and that for which we lust? Would it be best for our families if we reduced our expectations and allowed wives and mothers to return to being keepers of their homes?

Let me add here that I am painfully aware of our country's inflated economy and the epidemic divorce rate that may force some women to work outside of their homes. These women must work in order to survive and they have few, if any, luxuries. Some women work because it is truly their husband's leadership decision; others because their husbands are ill, disabled, or otherwise unable to work. Many more work because their fathers or husbands have abandoned them, or because they are widows and their children are unable or unwilling to help them.

The economy of our country, our very real needs, and many other factors make it difficult to give a definitive yes or no answer to the question as to whether a woman should or should not work outside her home. There are so many varied situations to consider – there are the women who are unmarried, married without children, married with children, and a growing number of single mothers. There may even be extenuating circumstances and variations within those groups. Rather than state a dogmatic position for all women, I have chosen to provide a few guidelines to be considered, as well as to discuss some of the distinct disadvantages that a woman must consider if she chooses to enter the workplace. This chapter is meant to provide you with enough information to evaluate objectively whether you should work outside your home or not.

Considerations for an Unmarried Woman

Many young women today believe they are intellectually capable of handling advanced types of work required in our modern society. This may be somewhat true, but there are numerous physical and spiritual disadvantages in certain occupations. Even the educational preparation for most careers exposes young women to deceptive influences.

No matter what the subject is, the curriculums used in college courses today provide an education that is focused almost entirely on the humanistic philosophy of life. In order to pass her exams a young woman will be required to absorb information that will oppose her Christian way of life. This fact can develop a dichotomy of thinking within a young woman's mind and put a tremendous strain on her ability to resist satanic deception. I am not saying that a young person cannot remain true to Christ in such a situation. However, she would need to possess advanced Biblical knowledge and be exceptionally mature spiritually to survive the anti-Christian impact on her thinking. Most young women are not equipped with the essential maturity required to be able to resist the web of deception that is woven into humanistic education today.

There is also a problem with the numerous career choices available to women today. Frankly, many of the careers women chose are not compatible with God's design for womanhood. An occupation that is not in agreement with God's design is any line of work that would require a woman to compete against men for a controlling position. Such an occupation creates a working atmosphere that is in opposition to creation's order and places an insufferable strain on both sexes. Under these circumstances a man must treat his woman co-worker as if she were just another man. My husband has spoken with many policemen who must constantly battle to overcome their feelings of protectiveness toward their female partners.

Equally damaging is when a woman hardens her own femininity for the sake of a career. In doing so she is in danger of becoming headstrong, willful, and self-serving as she strives to compete with men for the sake of her own advancement. Developing such characteristics may aid a woman for competing in today's workplace, but these traits also make it very difficult for her to remain truly feminine. A woman who becomes accustomed to debating and challenging men all day at work will find it difficult to then be submissive to her husband in the evening.

An unmarried Christian woman should always consider the effect of her education and occupation on the success of a future marriage. Before choosing any occupation, a Biblical woman ought to seek God's purpose for the talents He has bestowed upon her. A woman who desires God to be first in her life will want to use those talents in a manner that will be pleasing to Him. She must be especially alert to any deceptive influence that Satan might use in order to lead her away from God's design for womanhood.

As a general rule if an unmarried Christian woman decides to venture into the workplace, she should choose employment that will exercise her talents, but will not destroy her feminine characteristics. Unless she believes God calls her to a life of Christian service and celibacy, she should consider only those occupations that will help prepare her for, but not hinder her from, her future role as wife and mother. Nursing, teaching, food preparation, artistic endeavors, and clerical work are just a few examples of employment that might enhance a woman's feminine role. However, it remains true that most of the curriculum in our modern colleges and universities contains humanistic philosophy. A woman who chooses this route will need to be vigilant in her relationship with Christ.

Considerations for a Married Woman Without Children

Many young ladies are already working when they enter marriage. This is considered by most modern women to be advantageous in today's economy. These women believe that work experience may be essential if a woman is widowed, or if her husband becomes disabled or otherwise unable to support their family. However, does a Christian woman need to panic about preparing for the possibility of a future disaster, or can she trust that God will prepare her sufficiently if the need arises? This is a question of trust that each individual woman must consider before the Lord.

Despite the monetary advantages, there are also some distinct disadvantages for a wife who has an occupation outside the home. When a woman weds she elects a lifetime career as her husband's helpmate; therefore, when she works outside her home she has two careers. A wife with a career will constantly have an emotional struggle between her job, her boss's demands, and her role as her husband's helpmate. She must be especially careful not to form a wife-like loyalty to her boss.

A Biblical woman's first responsibility before God is to be a helpmate to her husband. Therefore, she will want any work that she does to be secondary to that first calling. The optimum situation for a Biblical woman is that her work will aid and encourage (but not replace) her husband's responsibility for providing for the family. Ideally, any work she does outside the home would be with her husband rather than in separate careers. The wives of farmers, men who own their own businesses, or missionaries and pastors find it natural to work with their husbands. It is not possible for every woman to work directly with her husband, but no matter what else she does it is vital that she remains under his leadership and protection.

Perhaps the greatest disadvantage for the working wife is that her occupation may cause her to develop completely separate goals apart from her husband. This separation creates a conflict of interest with a wife's role as helpmate and will leave her with little time or energy to a develop a oneness of purpose with her husband. Couples with separate aspirations in life may meet occasionally as they rush out the door to their own events, but neither will play a very active role in the goals of the other. As a result, their relationship becomes more like roommates rather than husband and wife. This is hardly a picture of the oneness that God designed for a wife to build with her husband.

Considerations for a Woman With Children

It is my personal conviction that a Biblical woman with children should make any sacrifice possible to be a full-time helpmate, mother, and keeper of the home. In 1990 a survey of 1000 households in southern California encouraged me to believe that most working mothers share my conviction. This study revealed that, "80% of the mothers in the survey said they would quit their jobs, if they could, to raise their children at home." The survey also stated that, "many respondents said they cannot live up to their ideals of even the most mundane family traditions, such as eating dinner together." Some social historians went on to say that the "findings reflect a 'new realism' about the financial and emotional toll that an 80-hour workweek inflicts on dual-earner families. We've reached a time when we're more realistic of what the costs are of full-time employment for two-earner families."[20] Although this particular study was done over 10 years ago, I have since witnessed similar reports in recent newscasts. Even highly paid professional women are now discovering that their careers are less fulfilling than they originally thought; and that their children are suffering because of mother's absence.

This information is both sad and happy news. It is sad because it means that the women who forsook home and children thinking they were house-slaves have now discovered that they are work-slaves — trapped in a life-style they have difficulty escaping. It is happy news because it means that some women are recognizing the importance of motherhood and they are seeking ways to return home. Perhaps future generations will see the negative consequences of a dual-career family and look more favorably at the need for mothers to remain at home with their children.

As I said previously there may be several reasons that Christian mothers must work and I deeply sympathize with these women because of the stress that they must bare. Much prayer and study of God's Word is needed in order for a working mother to be able to bear her multiple burdens. Careful planning, time management, and God's gracious help will enable a woman who has no other choice but to remain employed.

For those mothers who do have a choice, may I appeal to you to reconsider your priorities? There is no greater calling for a woman than the privilege of being a mother, but this privilege also carries grave responsibilities. A mother has elected to undertake a very demanding and time-consuming career – one that includes her influence in her children's lives, both present and future. This career requires the same devotion and dedication as any other occupational choice. Sacrifice, long-term commitment, hard work, time, and a variety of skills are required to be a successful mother. Children desperately need their own mother's full-time love and guidance in their lives. Saving any one of your children from drugs or a promiscuous life-style is worth any personal sacrifice.

Warning

If you are a working wife and mother, do not use this book as your excuse to quit your job without planning and discussion with your husband. Do not make such a leadership decision by yourself! There may be extenuating circumstances that must be resolved before it is possible for you to return home.

When a wife works outside the home the family becomes accustomed to what appears to be additional income. Actually debts are often incurred simply *because* the wife's income allows them. Once you and your husband are used to a life-style afforded by two salaries, it is very difficult to make a sudden change. Change is only possible if together you agree to reduce your debts and adjust your life-style in order to live within your husband's salary alone. In most cases where there is a will there is a way; but this way could take from six months to two years to fully accomplish.

The wife who wishes to stay home with her children should do some homework before she even approaches her husband with the idea of quitting her job. Careful planning, respectful presentation of that plan, and resourcefulness on a wife's part may be all it takes for her husband's enthusiastic endorsement of her homecoming.

Few women have careers that have high salaries; most have jobs that barely cover the expenses incurred due to their work. Therefore, the first thing a working mother might do is to calculate just how much money she actually brings home after expenses. I have seen several cases where both the husband and wife were shocked at how little money the wife actually contributed to their total income. A woman who was a real estate broker and earned $40,000 a year told of her experience. Her CPA pointed out that she was paying 60% of her salary to federal and state income taxes, social security tax, and other work-related expenses. After she subtracted the cost of her extra clothing, childcare, meals out, and other sundries required by her job, she found that she cleared only $8,000 per year. This revelation caused her to stop selling real estate and to engage in a home-style cottage industry. With her children's help she made arts and crafts and sold them at local swap meets. After expenses and taxes she netted $9,000 her first year, *plus* she was available to her husband and her children on a full time basis.

There are many possibilities for families who truly need extra income. Some creative women have begun home businesses like the woman in our illustration above. An added benefit has been that many of these enterprises have turned into family affairs. Other women have employers who have allowed them to telecommute. Some have found that what they and their children gain from home schooling is worth the sacrifice of the little that they earned, and certainly less expensive than day care and private schools.

Another Important Warning

If you have a strong conviction that you need to be meeting the needs of your children at home, but your husband is unwilling to make this sacrifice, then it will be necessary for you to continue to work. A situation such as this will be a difficult test of your character as you attempt to maintain a submissive attitude toward your husband's decision. God can use this situation to help you develop a deeper dependency on Him. Pray that He will help you maintain a correct Biblical attitude and that He will reveal to your husband both the need and the means for you to be at home training your children.

Some Questions to Ask Yourself

The following are a few basic questions that any woman may ask herself in order to determine whether her work is in keeping with God's design for Biblical womanhood.

1. Is my work in keeping with God's design and His stated will for women and their relationship with men? Must I sacrifice His will to pursue my line of work?

2. What is my motivation? Do I work because of personal ambition, a desire for recognition, or for riches? Do I work because it is God's plan for my life?

3. Does my job place me in danger of being influenced by false and deceptive philosophies for life?

4. Must I sacrifice godly femininity for the sake of career advancement?

5. Have I sought my husband's (or my father's) leadership concerning my work?

6. Does my work cause me to defy my husband's lead and prevent me from being his helpmate?

7. Does my work create separation and friction between my husband and myself?

8. Does my work strengthen or weaken my husband's desire to be a Biblical leader, protector, and provider?

9. Does my work reflect responsiveness to my husband's leadership and does it fulfill his need for a helpmate?

10. Does my work interfere with my responsibility to aid my husband in teaching and training our children?

If you must answer contrary to commonsense or the Biblical position to even one of these questions, your marriage relationship and your children may be suffering. If this is the case, I pray that God will reveal the way that you might remedy your situation. May you have God's peace as you endeavor to live according to Biblical womanhood – whether you work in or outside of your home.

CHAPTER XIX

KEEPERS OF THE HOME

I was born in 1940 just a year and a half before Pearl Harbor. My grandfathers had both lived through World War I and they and my parents had survived the Great Depression. Throughout my early childhood, I remember that Christian principles were the essence of the American way of life. There was no objection to having prayer in our schools or the fact that every Christmas my grade school recognized the birth of Jesus. Some women worked, but it was generally accepted that a mother's home was her workplace.

No one that I knew was rich, but our mothers' were still able to make meals from simple ingredients and we never went hungry. They also found ways to turn even modest houses into warm and comfortable homes. It was a time in our history when women understood that homemaking was much more than just cleaning a house and cooking meals. Although material possessions were few, home was where family and friends gathered for fellowship and children were trained for life. The typical American home was not rich in prosperity, but for the most part the people within it were rich in character and moral values. However, within a few short years of my birth, things rapidly began to change.

One of my seventh grade requirements was to write a thesis on the career of my choice. However, wife, mother, and homemaker were not career options from which I could choose. Our schools still taught home economics classes, but the girls of my generation were mainly being educated for careers and in essence encouraged to forsake full-time homemaking. This trend continued until now, fifty years later, most schoolgirls have working mothers and they believe that they too will have lifetime careers outside their homes. The modern houses these girls live in are no longer the center of family life nor are they the principle location where moral values are taught and upheld.

Today, a large number of houses stand empty for the majority of the day. With no keeper of the home present, these modern houses stand as unguarded, empty shells that provide families with little more than places to eat and sleep. Latchkey children return from school to nothing more than cold electronics as substitute parents. These children learn negative lessons about life from television and the influence of their friends, rather than receive positive direction from real life moms. They heat a snack in a microwave, rather than help Mom prepare dinner. They desire to fit in with their peers more than with parents who are responsible for training their souls. Modern homes may be rich in prosperity, but so many children today are poor in character.

When there were keepers at home our nation's young people understood the meaning of integrity, they respected their elders, and were taught to be polite to others. Now it seems that respect and honor toward others are foreign concepts to many of the young people who will form the future of our nation.

I am sure there are many more reasons for the drastic change of attitudes toward motherhood, homemaking, and moral values that have taken place in just my lifetime. Certainly one major reason has been the influence of humanistic philosophy, as previously discussed. However, two other important reasons may be:

1. Many women have lost their understanding of how important homemaking is to their families' welfare and/or,

2. They do not possess the patience and self-discipline to work at home.

Homemakers Wanted!

Many things have changed since I was a child, but one thing has not. Most women still continue to do the majority of the housekeeping chores. Some women believe that they have fallen heir to the cooking and cleaning by default. However, the real reason a woman is inclined to oversee the needs within a home is because God designed her for and appointed her to that position. She was created to be a helpmate to her husband, life-giver and teacher to her children, and the keeper of the home environment.

> *That they may teach the young women to be sober, to love their husbands, to love their children, To be discreet, chaste, keepers at home, good, obedient to their own husbands, that the word of God be not blasphemed* (Titus 2:4-5).

God made it very clear that being a homemaker is important when he instructed older women to teach younger women to be keepers at home. However, for the past several generations, young women have not been taught that homemaking is an art worthy of pursuit. I know I was not. I became a latchkey child at the age of twelve.

After my mother went into the workplace, my family's weekends changed from a time of rest to a time of stress. My poor, harassed mother tried to delegate a week's worth of work in just a few hours each weekend. There was little time to convey to me that homemaking was a worthwhile pursuit. All I knew about homemaking was that it was tedious work worthy of avoidance whenever possible.

Every woman wants to know that her labor is for a good cause. A woman who wishes to be a teacher will spend years in order to obtain a teaching degree. She will work hard at being a good teacher because she believes that others will benefit from her efforts. Similarly, a young wife needs to understand that homemaking is valuable to her family's welfare. I pray that God will use this book to help young Christian women understand that homemaking is an honorable pursuit in His eyes.

Several generations of mothers have neglected to teach their daughters the joy of homemaking. Therefore, the fulfillment one can receive from creating a pleasant home is virtually unknown to most modern young women. Nevertheless, there are books, magazines, and some older women who can teach younger women how to care for their homes. However, I believe the greatest obstacle to the enjoyment of homemaking is a lack of self-discipline.

Only the Self-Disciplined Need Apply

Self-discipline, or self-control, is a hallmark of both human and spiritual maturity.

> *But the fruit of the Spirit is love, joy, peace, longsuffering, kindness, goodness, faithfulness, gentleness, temperance* (Galatians 5:22-23).
> (The Greek word used for temperance means self-control.)

An individual learns the art of self-discipline by exercising self-control in order to overcome a weakness, to accomplish a difficult task, and to reach a greater goal. A teacher who enjoys teaching, but dislikes paperwork, must discipline herself in order to grade her students' test papers and record the results. Exercising self-control benefits both the teacher and her students. First, the teacher becomes a more mature individual. Second, her students benefit because their test scores help the teacher measure their progress and acquaint her with the areas where they may need further training. Similarly, a woman benefits when she exercises self-control as she learns to do the work of homemaking. She gains the self-control (a measure of maturity) while her family benefits by having their emotional and physical needs met.

A dedicated teacher does not equate teaching with only the drudgery of paperwork, and a wife should not equate homemaking with only the work of cleaning. Homemaking includes some work that is pleasant and other tasks that are not fun at all. A woman may love to cook, but hate to clean the stove afterwards. Nevertheless, she does the cleaning because she knows it is important for the health and welfare of her family. Without the proper nutrition and sanitation her family would be constantly ill. Therefore, a wife and mother will do the things that she enjoys and if necessary she will discipline herself to accomplish the less enjoyable tasks. Chores that are less than entertaining require self-discipline to accomplish, whether that work is done inside or outside the home.

Warning

One of the problems with teaching any principle is that some people may be extreme in their practice of that principle. There are at least three possible homemaking excesses of which I am aware: the woman whose house is more important than the people who live in it; the woman who is a slave to others; and the woman who tries to avoid both of the two extremes.

The woman who is obsessive about housekeeping will try to keep "her" house looking as if no one lives in it. This woman will become very upset if someone walks on "her" carpet after she has vacuumed. The woman who is a slave to others believes that housekeeping is her job alone and she denies her children training in domestic chores. By her attitude, this woman encourages her husband and children to treat her as their personal maid. Meanwhile, the third woman goes to the opposite extreme. She thinks that anything and everything else is of higher priority than a neat home. She rarely does housework and she even more rarely trains her children to do household duties. All of these extremes are examples of imbalanced viewpoints toward homemaking.

Being a balanced, Biblical homemaker does not mean that a wife is the only one in the house who is able to vacuum a room or cook a meal. A wife may be the primary cook and bottle washer, but her husband and children should also know how to do the laundry, clean a bathroom and kitchen, and care for themselves. (A husband **should** know how to take care of himself, but please remember another Biblical principle – it is not a wife's place to try to pressure her husband to do even that which he should do.) A mother should also remember that part of the Biblical reason she is expected to be a keeper of the home is so she can train her children for their adult lives. This includes teaching both boys and girls to take over their own physical maintenance and to be able to do house and yard work as young as is reasonable.

Yes, But …

"Yes, homemaking is important to the welfare of the family, but …" What follows the "but" is usually something that seems to be a logical objection as to why a woman need not choose homemaking. Most modern women believe that a wife has the right to choose between homemaking and working outside the home, regardless of God's Word, her family's needs, or any other factor. However, God's Word says that a wife is to be a "keeper at home;" therefore, a Christian woman who has chosen marriage and motherhood has already made her choice. Any work that she does outside her home is in addition to, and lesser in priority to her homemaking responsibilities. A wife cannot escape her Biblical role as homemaker with, "Yes, but…" answers. Nevertheless, because "yes, but …" is so prevalent among young women, it is necessary to discuss at least two such objections. They are:

1. "Yes, but I am not the domestic type."

2. "Yes, but I am too talented, intelligent, and outgoing to 'just stay home' all day and be 'only' a wife and mother.

Let us analyze these two objections.

The First Objection: "I am not the domestic type."

First, a woman is the domestic type simply by virtue of being born a woman. God designed women to be "nesters." Of the two sexes, women are normally the ones who intrinsically care about decorating their homes and they are the first to think of the physical needs of their families (proper nutrition, clothing, and health). Almost every bachelor's apartment I have ever seen desperately needed a "woman's touch," and their refrigerators contained little more than sandwich makings, moldy cheese, sour milk, and soda drinks. Most men appear to be perfectly satisfied with a comfortable chair, sheets covering the windows, and pizza for breakfast. (My husband says that men would be happy living in a cave as long as it was wired for a television and stereo and there was a sports car parked outside.) Women naturally care about houses, furniture, pretty curtains, and a balanced diet.

Some women might say that they are not the domestic type as a plausible-sounding excuse for being inexperienced in the skills of homemaking. However, when a woman understands that being the keeper of the home is an important job, she can learn the skills required for the job. There is a list of recommended reading for learning such skills at the end of this chapter. Knowledge, self-discipline, and on-the-job experience will also increase a woman's enjoyment of homemaking and ease any house keeping phobias.

It must be noted here that making a home is not a cookie cutter sort of art where all homemakers must display the same proficiency in every area. For instance, one woman may love to sew all of her children's clothing, while providing her family very simple meals. For another woman, the tiny details of sewing make her extremely nervous, so her sewing is limited to mending only when necessary. But, she may spend a lot of time cooking because her husband loves gourmet cuisine. Both women should know the basics of the arts of sewing and cooking, but their individual talents, their husband's tastes, and their families specific needs will direct each one to have a different homemaking emphasis.

Second Objection: "Yes, but I am too talented ..."

"Yes, but I am too talented (etc.) to just stay home and be only a wife and mother." The phrases "just stay home" and "only" reveal that some women think homemaking and being a mother have little value. Furthermore, it implies that only those women who are shy, have no talent, and possess very little intelligence could possibly choose to work at home. However, God never said for women to just stay home and vegetate. The homemaker of Proverbs 31 looked after her home, but she never "just" stayed home.

She looketh well to the ways of her household, and eateth not the bread of idleness (Proverbs 31:27).

Certainly, no one who has studied Proverbs 31 could accuse this woman of a lack of talent or intelligence, nor could they say that she was "only" a wife and mother. (See **Chapter X.**)

When a woman quits forming sentences that begin with "Yes, but..." and when she disciplines herself to do the work of homemaking, both she and her family will physically benefit. However, there is an added benefit that is just as important. A keeper at home is also close at hand when her family and friends are most in need of help.

1 Timothy 5:3-10 reveals that a keeper of the home includes activities that offer physical, emotional, and spiritual help to her family as well as others outside her home. Although this passage discusses the conditions under which the church may help a widow, it also provides us with information about what God values most in a woman. 1 Timothy 5:4, 8, and 16 state that a widowed woman is to be assisted first by her family, but that the church is to help if she does not have a family to care for her. However, the church helps her only if she meets certain qualifications. A widow's trust in God, her personal character (Verses 6, 7, and 9), and works such as those below are all part of her qualifications.

> *Let not a widow be taken into the number under threescore years old, having been the wife of one man, Well reported of for good works; if she have brought up children, if she have lodged strangers, if she have washed the saints' feet, if she have relieved the afflicted, if she have diligently followed every good work*
> (1 Timothy 5:9-10).

There are other scriptural illustrations of homemakers helping others through the skills they learned as homemakers (not through meddling or self-righteous crusades). The women who housed and fed the disciples, traveling believers, the Apostles, and Christ Himself are examples of homemakers who were available to serve a ministry. After Jesus healed Peter's ailing mother-in-law, she rose and ministered to Him (Matthew 8:14-15). Women such as *Mary, the mother of John, whose surname was Mark* (Acts 12:12), opened their homes for early church meetings. Dorcus is an example of a woman who helped care for widows in her community. Before Peter raised Dorcus from her death bed, *the widows stood by him weeping, and showing the coats and garments which Dorcus made, while she was with them* (Acts 9:39b).

Balanced homemakers are valuable assets not only to their families but to their churches and communities as well. The 1 Timothy widow, as well as the Proverbs 31 wife, worked to fulfill their roles as helpmates and mothers. Their families benefited, but so did strangers, believers, and the needy. These women were successful Biblical women because they applied their minds and their talents to the role that God had designed for them.

A keeper at home is a woman whose "home-office" is located in a house. Yes, she has certain housework responsibilities. She should cook meals that please her husband, do laundry, vacuum and mop floors, and create a home environment as pleasant as possible. More than anyone else she sets the atmosphere of her family's home and how she keeps it has an effect on all who enter her door. However, a homemaker is more than a housekeeper. She is also privileged to teach her children moral and spiritual lessons about life and she has the ability to mend feelings that have been hurt by the world better than any doctor. Furthermore, a keeper at home is her children's living example of Biblical womanhood and her husband's ready companion. She is available when her neighbors are ill or when the widowed need her help.

A modern woman can be a successful keeper of the home as well. God gave her special talents and then He said for her to exercise those talents within and out from her home base. If she feels limited it may be from not knowing how to be a homemaker or it may simply be her own lack of willingness to apply herself to her God-given role. Lack of knowledge can be remedied, but the woman herself must overcome any lack of willingness.

Recommended Reading

Is There Life After Housework? Don Aslett's Cleaning Center, 311 S. 5th Ave., Pocatello, Idaho 83201, 1-800-451-2402

Sidetracked Home Executives – From Pigpen to Paradise by Pam Young and Peggy Jones.

Emilie's Creative Home Organizer by Emilie Barnes. Published by Harvest House Publishers, Eugene, Oregon.

CHAPTER XX

A WOMAN'S MINISTRY

Before the missionary began talking he glanced at the audience of eager young faces awaiting his speech. He knew that many of them dreamed of becoming missionaries someday. They anticipated hearing how exhilarating it is to lead souls to Christ in exotic far away countries. Then, he shocked his inexperienced audience and dispelled their romantic ideas about missionary life when he said: "If you lack the courage to go across the street to witness to your neighbor, what makes you think it will be any easier in a foreign nation?" This seasoned missionary knew the hardships, dangers, repeated rejections, and sorrows that were a reality on the mission field. He wisely stated, "Like charity, missionary work begins at home. Those who are not willing to sacrifice everything for the sake of Christ – should remain home." This is as true for a woman as it is for a missionary. If she is not willing to make the sacrifices that are required of a wife, she should remain unmarried!

Americans have long forgotten that home is a place of ministry. I too once viewed myself as "just" a wife and mother. I wrongly believed that the mundane things that I did for my husband and our children contributed little to mankind. I wanted to do something "more" important with my life.

I foolishly believed that God valued only highly visible crusades affecting millions of people. This romantic view of a ministry caused me to be guilty of diminishing the value of those people closest to me. Gratefully, the Lord led me to the realization that being a helpmate and mother is a very valuable ministry. In addition, He graciously made it clear to me that ministering to four very important people – my husband and my three children – was indeed my first calling.

My Own Ministry

The Bible reveals why God created the woman and how He expects her to live. What He says is of utmost importance; my opinions are inconsequential. Therefore, I have attempted throughout this book to refrain from using myself as an illustration. However, it occurred to me that the "life resume" of how God has used an ordinary woman like me might encourage other women to see their own lives from a different perspective. For this reason only do I share a little of the ministry that God has called me to do in my life.

My Husband – My Ministry

Even though my husband is actually a very private and quiet person, God has made him a dynamic leader as well. In order to lead most effectively he needs to be assured that all is well at home. He would be unable to apply his mind and energies properly to his calling if his home was in chaos. This means that I have a lot to do in order to assure him that all is well on the home front. Furthermore, my hard working husband needs a place where he can rest and escape from the stresses of his day. If I deny him a peaceful, orderly home then I increase his stress, not reduce it. One of the most important helpmate jobs I have is to create a restful home in which my husband actually desires to be.

Thousands of people have been helped by my husband's leadership abilities. His books, teaching, and the management of Christian companies have been instrumental in aiding many people to live Biblical lives. The work that I do also ministers to those same people, just in an indirect way. Like the head of a body my husband ministers directly; and like the muscles that keep the body strong, I minister behind the scenes. Though my work is mostly unseen by many people, my husband would not have the drive, time, or energy to do his work if I neglected mine.

I will never forget the day that Rick and I were sitting on our back porch. He was particularly quiet that day. His shoulders sagged a little and I knew he was greatly troubled by some difficulties at work. I said a silent prayer asking God to give him strength. A short while later, a beautiful hummingbird flew to the feeder that was hanging from the eaves of our house. We sat together silently watching one of God's little marvels. Then I remembered that Rick had recently hung a second feeder just outside our kitchen window. This prompted me to say, "Thank you for hanging the hummingbird feeder by the kitchen window. I just love watching the hummingbirds as I wash dishes and prepare dinner." My heavily burdened husband turned to me and said, "I love your enjoyment of the simple things of life. If it were not for you I would not have the strength to continue fighting the battles I must fight. It is because of you that I am able to carry on."

Dear reader you never know when some simple thing you say or do will bless your husband. No matter what your husband's job may be he still has battles to conquer. I pray my story will encourage you to minister to your husband so that God may use you to strengthen your husband during the conflicts in his life.

My Children – My Ministry

Although they are now adults, my husband and I shared an intense desire to help all three of our children become mature adults. God entrusted three precious lives to us, and we were accountable to Him to *"Train up a child in the way he should go..."* (Proverbs 22:16). God allowed me to see that training my children was actually ministering to the whole of mankind as well. Turning three people loose on the world, as undisciplined adults, would have been a sin against God as well as a gross injustice to my children and to our fellow man.

I must add here that no matter how well a mother trains her children they will never grow to sinless perfection – they will still be humans in need of a Savior. Your adult children will also face many trials in life and it is inevitable that you will feel great pain as you watch them struggle with those trials. But, words cannot express the joy a mother experiences when her children accept Jesus as their personal Savior. She will find no greater happiness in life than witnessing her adult children walking closely with Him. The pain she feels during the trials of their lives will be replaced by an immeasurable contentment as she watches them demonstrate godly integrity and strength of character. Dear ladies, your children are the heritage of your womb. You can leave no greater legacy than adult children who reflect the light of Christ in a dark and dying world.

A Resume of One Woman's Ministry

In almost fifty years of marriage, I have held numerous positions and done a variety of work. The following are some activities that have been part of my life's ministry.

1. Executive secretary and assistant to my husband's leadership: In this position I was responsible for budgeting,

organization of schedules, progress evaluation, and reports to "upper management."

2. Clerical work and bookkeeping: Did simple accounting and record keeping for two businesses and a home. I am the one who can locate last year's tax records and the box that contains birth certificates and safety deposit keys.

3. Volunteer: Worked part-time as a receptionist and record keeper for a husband and wife missionary team. Helped in a bookstore and volunteered in a hospital for a short period of time. Frequently filled in for vacationing secretaries and did other odd jobs in my husband's various businesses.

4. Money management: Acted as a Purchasing Agent, penny pincher, efficient shopper, and budget keeper. I have become an expert in stretching a dollar until it squeaks and have found bargains that were virtual give-aways.

5. School Administrator: My husband and I ran a private school for two years. With the aid of self-instructional curriculum, I worked as a teacher for twenty-three children, grades 1-12. I was also the record keeper, purchasing agent of curriculum and supplies, as well as the designer of forms and procedures for school operations.

6. Advisor: No psychologist can replace a wife and mother. She is a shoulder to cry on, a partner in laughter, an ear to strange and imaginative tales, and a prayer warrior with inside information. She encourages, admonishes, and exhorts her children. In addition she acts as a sounding board, assistant, supporter, and best friend to her husband.

7. Practical nurse: I bandaged, taped, painted funny red medicine faces on hurt knees, and kissed minor physical

injuries. Also, I made soup, orange juice, and read stories, sat up at night, rocked and otherwise nursed three children and a husband through a variety of illnesses.

8. Food Manager: In this capacity I was a dietitian, butcher, baker, chef and fast-food cook. I also planned, purchased, and prepared meals within a budget.

9. Housekeeper: Did laundry and cleaning. Yes, I did floors and windows as well as some other very messy and unpleasant jobs. I also headed and trained a staff of three assistants. These assistants became heads of their own departments as soon as they were able to manage their jobs.

10. Interior decorator: Painted walls and furniture, sewed curtains and bedspreads, and arranged furniture.

11. Seamstress: Clothing, doll and toy making, knitting, quilting, and other forms of needlework became my favorite specialties.

12. Hostess and Receptionist: Planned and prepared meals, served dinner parties, barbeques, and picnics. Acted as hostess for meetings and Bible studies, and opened our home as a hotel and diner for traveling friends.

13. Pioneer: Lived for over one year in a mountain cabin heated with coal or wood in a Ben Franklin stove. Hunted for berries and other wild edibles and tried rose hips tea, jelly, and syrup, as well as dandelion greens and other interesting things. I baked bread and boiled tough squirrel while I learned to "rough it" without fast-food hamburgers. I was forced to become an expert at improvisation when I forgot to buy some needed item on our weekly sixty-mile round-trip into town. In addition, I learned to cope with four feet deep snow, three children and one dog who had puppies, as well

as bears, raccoons, mountain lions, and other critters; five sets of down clothing, boots, and mittens drying by the stove, a cabin that could never be cleaned, and our first year of home schooling. (We did not live completely like pioneers. Water from the creek behind our cabin was pumped into the cabin by a generator and all we had to do was keep the ice chopped away from the lines – and pray. We had electricity for lights and cooking as well as a telephone – unless of course they failed during bad weather, which was often. We also had a four-wheel drive truck that I frequently got stuck in snowdrifts, or slid into a ditch and mailbox.)

14. And finally, an author: I am now revising this book which I wrote twelve years ago and this is the miracle of all miracles, accomplished only by the grace of God. He has taken a painfully shy person and allowed her to participate in a ministry to other women. His wonders never cease!

Not all women are alike. Each woman possesses her own unique talents and her husband has his own needs. However, whether a woman's husband is a business executive, a master mechanic, or a salesman, he still needs the backing and support of his helpmate in order to be a successful employee, husband, father, church, and community member. And, a woman's children need their mother's love, care, and training. Beyond these two important ministries a woman who has the energy, time, talent, and leadership of her husband, can also minister to others. The following are just a few suggestions where a woman might use her talents to minister to the needs of others outside of her home.

Administrator

A woman who has a gift or talent for administration might organize a network of helps in her church (with the approval and leadership involvement of her pastor) or neighborhood. She could organize groups of women who would be willing to minister to specific needs, such as a group of women to be prayer warriors, or a group who would provide transportation for the elderly or disabled. Then, when the need arises the organizer could call upon prearranged volunteers to fill that specific need. In this way prayer, meals, cleaning, transportation, visitation, babysitting, and much more could be provided quickly to the sick or needy. Another possibility for the woman who is talented in administration is to begin a home business with her husband and children.

Teacher

A woman could home school her own children, and/or tutor other children from families who are unable to do it themselves. She could teach other interested women one of her own talents, such as painting or organizing time. Another possibility is to train other women in homemaking skills such as canning, sewing, baking, or money management.

Artist

An artistic and creative woman could write, paint, sculpt, play music, or sing to the glory of God. She might also consider sharing her talent with others by teaching or through performances.

Helps

Many women are needed to assist administrators. A woman could provide physical help such as meals, babysitting, cleaning, and transportation to those in need. She could help her pastor and his family at stressful times or volunteer at hospitals, rest homes, or political campaigns. A church always has many needs a woman can fill: welcoming new people, making or distributing cassette tapes of the pastor's lessons to shut-ins, helping in the nursery, cleaning the church, or being prayer warriors, to name just a few.

Hospitality and Fellowship

A woman could organize other women for Bible studies, luncheons, and other fellowship gatherings. She could form a group to exchange meals once a week or once a month. She might open her home to church or community functions, traveling missionaries, or other Christian speakers. She could also offer fellowship to the very shy, invalid, and other needy people who would be otherwise isolated and alone.

Older Woman

The older woman usually has talents and many years of practical experience that would serve well the members of her church. She is especially needed to teach younger women how to be sensible, pure, kind, and lovers of their children and husbands (Titus 2:4-5).

The opportunities for an older woman to minister to younger women are abundant. Most young women today are victims of a lack of parental training in self-control, contentment, frugality, homemaking skills, and parenting responsibilities – all of which are needed in the ministries of wife and mother. Frequently, these young women have come from homes where their mothers worked or felt trapped and resented their roles. As a result, the skills involved in making a warm home have become a lost art and the unselfish service of charity, wife, and mother a lost cause. This situation has created the false opinion among younger women in this country that being a homemaker means doing nothing and being bored. How desperately we need older women who will teach younger women the skills of homemaking.

The list you have just read contains only a few of the many possibilities where a woman might minister to others. It takes creativity, ingenuity, and imagination as well as dedication, self-discipline, and plain hard work to be a ministering helpmate, mother, homemaker, church, and community member. How a woman cares for the needs of others depends entirely on whether she will use the mind and the talents that God gave her, or whether she will limit herself by closing her mind to the wide range of choices she has. A woman should always keep in mind, however, that God never leads her into any service that opposes her husband's leadership or denies his rightful needs. A grand and glorious ministry may get a woman applause and recognition from the world (or even in her church), but if it becomes more important than her husband, home, and children, it is not God's leading, nor does it bring Him glory. Any woman, who forsakes those within her home in favor of a ministry outside of it, causes her home to lie empty, her husband to struggle without his helpmate, and her children to live as if they were orphans.

You are a woman with at least one unique talent – praise God! By all means share your talent with your family and others. Never let vain philosophers convince you that your role is unimportant or allow the enemy to lead you astray from God's purpose for giving you a talent. You are intelligent – praise God! Use your intelligence to think of all the possibilities that are available within His design. Do not waste His gift by chasing after things that oppose His plan for womanhood. If you also are outgoing and personable, again praise God. Allow Him to use you in a way that will bring glory to His name. If you will do so then whatever you do will have meaning and value beyond this world. May God bless you abundantly in the ministry in which you chose to be involved.

CHAPTER XXI

TO LOVE THEIR CHILDREN

Everyone seems to understand that it is intrinsic to a woman's nature to love and protect her children. There are even several English idioms that describe a woman's natural love for her progeny. One such idiom is "motherly love." Another is "mother tiger," which aptly describes how even the tiniest woman will become like a roaring tiger if she perceives that her child is under attack. A "mother tiger" will stand between a dangerous situation and her offspring without the slightest thought for her own safety. However, since it apparently is natural for a woman to love her children, why does God specifically declare that older women are to teach younger women *"to love their children?"*

> *That they may teach the young women . . . to*
> *love their children* (Titus 2:4).

The only possible answer to this question is that the love in Titus 2:4 is a different form of love than the nurturing, protective love that a woman may naturally possess. This chapter will explain the special kind of love that must be learned, after first analyzing the characteristics of a mother's natural love.

Natural, Motherly Love

Within hours of birth, a mother and child are able to begin a rudimentary system of communication and response. This system starts with the baby's first cry. Crying is the vocabulary whereby an infant communicates his or her needs, wants, or state of being. For instance, all newborns have a hungry cry and a distress cry. It does not take long for even a first time mother to learn the difference between these two types of crying. Furthermore, by four to six weeks of age infants are able to control their vocal cords and they are cognizant enough to communicate frustration, as well as that counterfeit cry that is actually a demand for attention.[21] A mother's natural sensitivity to her child enables her to interpret the infant's cries, noises, and gestures; and motherly love prompts her to respond to her child's needs.

There is no question that natural motherly love exists and that it is necessary for the physical welfare of an infant baby. However, as important as this responsive type of love is to a baby, it alone is not enough to train a child in becoming a mature adult.

Responsiveness in a mother is valuable, but it can also be fallible. It is fallible because responsiveness originates in the emotions. Emotional reactions act on cue to a stimulus. They are void of thoughtful planning or long-ranged discernment. Responsive love is important while an infant needs total care and protection. However, it can be extremely detrimental when a mother's emotional reactions prevent an older child from learning the harsher realities of life. A mother's sympathetically driven love can cause an older child to remain childish and prevent him from becoming a mature adult. The positive results every mother truly desires for her child requires a love that exceeds natural, motherly love.

The Love That Must Be Taught

The older woman is to teach a type of love that is based on the knowledge of what is best for a child from God's perspective. This love is mental, not emotional. It requires thinking about what is beneficial for the child's future, and is based on what a child needs in order to grow into a mature individual. It is not a shortsighted view of what his or her childish sin-nature wants or demands for the moment.

Many Scriptures clarify what is best to teach a child for his or her long-ranged benefit. For instance, in Proverbs 3:1 a mother admonishes her son to not forget her law and to keep her commandments. Her teaching is based on God's point of view and is not just for the child's current comfort. The major point of her teaching is for his future. Proverbs 3:2 explains that by following his mother's teaching God promises this son, *"length of days, and long life, and peace, shall they* (her law and commandments) *add to thee."* In verse 3 the mother further instructs her son to: *"Let not mercy and truth forsake thee: bind them about thy neck; write them upon the table of thine heart."* Her long-ranged purpose for this teaching is in verse 4, *"So shalt thou find favour and good understanding in the sight of God and man."* Further instructions follow in verses 5-7: *"Trust in the LORD with all thine heart; and lean not unto thine own understanding. In all thy ways acknowledge him, and he shall direct thy paths. Be not wise in thine own eyes: fear the LORD, and depart from evil."* Again, her teaching is mindful of her son's future as stated in verse 8: *"It shall be health to thy navel, and marrow to thy bones."*

A Titus 2:4 love requires acting and teaching in accordance with God's truth. A woman who loves in this manner will govern her child training by what God says is correct rather than by what just seems to be right to her at the moment.

"Older women" who understand Biblical truths are instructed to teach "younger women" how to love their children (Titus 2:4). They are to impart information about child training, as well as wisdom from their own successful results. Younger women need to be taught so their natural affections will be curbed and governed by truths.

It is impossible to cover the entire subject of how a mother should love her children in just one chapter. For a more thorough understanding of this complex and often emotional subject, I need to refer you to my husband's expertise. Rick's book, *What the Bible Says About ... Child Training*, is the most systematic development of Biblical child training information available. It is essential reading for any mother who wants to learn how to love her children Biblically. In the remainder of this chapter I will only emphasize the importance of the father's involvement in child training.

I hear many complaints from today's mothers about their husbands' lack of involvement in child training. What can a wife do to encourage her husband to become more involved? The answer is simple: be a submissive wife, respect your husband's leadership, and do not interfere when he attempts to train the children. I cannot over stress how harmful it is for children to see their mother have a non-submissive and disrespectful attitude toward their father. If she openly challenges his child-training decisions or instructions, she is overtly teaching her children to be rebels. The mother who does this is actively destroying her children's respect for both herself and their father. Such an attitude is counterproductive to the role of helpmate and never gives a father incentive to increase his involvement in child training.

Parental Disunity

My husband has counseled with many parents who were having serious problems with their children. Incorrect child training techniques could easily be solved, but he found that if the parents were not unified, his counseling would fall on deaf ears. Rick often had to first do marriage counseling before he could help the parents with the problems they were having with their children. One of the biggest obstacles to proper child training, and the most damaging to children, is the disunity of their parents. Although, a father can be equally to blame for this parenting dilemma, this book is addressed to women so I will only address those things that a wife may do to promote parental disunity.

A mother's natural love and her desire to nurture her child can come into direct conflict with the father's objectives to train their child toward maturity. (It might be beneficial at this point to review **Chapter VIII**, **"When Two Heads Are Better Than One."**) Whenever a mother feels that the father is being unfair or too strict, her protective nature may bristle. For instance, she may feel the father is unfair if he demands that their unwilling son mow the lawn on a hot day. Or, she may feel that he is too strict if he requires a sobbing daughter to pay for a carelessly broken vase with the money she saved for a special dress.

Perhaps the mother feels that her son's comfort on a hot day or her daughter's emotions are more important than a mowed lawn or an inconsequential vase. The father probably is not really concerned about having the lawn mowed on exactly that day or that the vase is ever replaced. More than likely he has a different objective in mind. What may concern him more than the children's comfort is that they learn valuable lessons for their rapidly approaching adult lives. He desires for the son to learn that work must be done even when it is uncomfortable, and he wants his daughter to learn that there are always consequences for her careless actions. Sometimes a mother's protectiveness causes her to misunderstand the underlying reasons for her husband's child-training decisions. If she allows her desire to protect her children and interferes with the father's directives, she can prevent her children from receiving some valuable character lessons. One of the best ways to keep a father uninvolved is for the mother to interfere with his child training decisions.

A mother's natural protectiveness will cause her to feel that her husband's treatment of "her" children is at least occasionally unfair. However, whether or not her assessment is correct is really not the important issue. What is crucial is that the children learn to be respectful and obedient to their father's instructions, even when those instructions go against a mother's special sensitivity. Almost the cruelest thing a mother can do to her children is openly to challenge the father's instructions or correction. (Of course, a mother **must** protect her child against true abuse. However, she should not interfere when something her husband does just seems unfair to her.) **A child can get over an occasional unfairness, but he will suffer more severely from lessons of disrespect learned from his mother.** I repeat: there may be nothing more harmful to a child's future than having his or her mother interfere with their father's training. Let us look at some of the things a mother can teach her children just by the way she treats her husband's child-training decisions.

Do You Know What Your Children Are Learning?

Children are very observant. They learn from watching how their parents live their lives. For instance, they learn to respect or to disrespect their father by watching their mother's responses to his leadership decisions and directions. A wife's cooperation (or lack thereof) will silently teach her children more lessons than her words could ever teach. Some of these lessons are as follows:

1. A wife can passively or actively interfere with her husband's instructions to their children. Passive interference might be in the form of forgetfulness. For instance, when she disagrees with her husband's instructions, she may "forget" to oversee the children's compliance. Her lack of submission will teach the children to also "forget" whenever they wish to get out of obeying any authority. This tactic can backfire on mother because the children will "forget" to follow her instructions as well.

Active interference is evident anytime a wife openly argues against, or defies, the father's instructions. The children will quickly follow mother's lead and they too will defy their father's authority. And, do not think that children cannot hear whispered disrespect, or read body language such as hateful facial expressions and resentful sighs – they can! When children get even the slightest sense that their mother does not agree with their father they will quickly learn to pit their parents against one another. This age-old" divide and conquer" technique is one that children often use in order to escape a command they would rather not obey.

On the other hand, a mother's cooperation with the father's instructions will teach the children to respect and obey their father. As the children observe their mother's pleasantly submissive attitude toward the father's authority, they learn to respect all other forms of authority as well. Respect for authority is one of the most important truths for children to learn. It affects their relationship with God, with government and laws, with employers, and is central to God's plan for marriage.

2. A wife needs her husband's firmness in order to train their children, especially in the teen years. How effective a

father will be very often depends on whether his wife taught the children to obey their father during their preteen years. When a mother challenges a father's right of authority, she completely destroys his future effectiveness with the children. However, when she teaches them to respect their father while they are young, they will be more likely to listen to what he says when they are older.

3. A daughter watches her mother's example of how to treat her future husband. By watching mother's reaction to the father's decisions, she either learns how to be a supportive helpmate or she learns to be defiant and self-willed, just like her mother. Your daughter's present attitude toward her father is a mirror image of what she has observed and learned from you. Her future husband will either be blessed by what she has learned or he will be afflicted with a willful wife. Good or bad, she is learning by observing her mother's attitude toward her father.

4. A son also learns about authority by observing his mother. When he is required to respect his father's position as head of the household, he learns to respect other positions of authority in general. A son who understands authority will grow up to be a stronger leader himself. However, when the father allows his wife to show him disrespect and bows to her rebellion, his son will grow up to be weak like his father, or he will grow to dislike his father for that weakness. A grown man who was ashamed of his father's weakness often fears that he too will be a weak man. In order to keep from appearing weak, that son may someday compensate by being over-bearing on his own wife and family.

During his early, impressionable years a boy's mother is his major example of womanhood. Whatever he observes in mom is what he will later attribute to all women. A son who witnesses his mother's rebellious attitude invariably disrespects all women. Perhaps this is because he inherently knows that rebellion is incorrect.

A mother who loves her children with a Titus 2:4 love understands the necessity of restricting her natural, motherly responses when her child's long-ranged benefit is at stake. Even when she feels that her husband is too strict, insensitive to her child's feelings, or unfair in his reprimands, this mother knows that her child's respectful attitude towards his father is far more valuable than how he might presently feel. Without early training and respect for the father, that seemingly sweet and sensitive child can become a self-willed, angry, hateful, and rebellious teen – and his mother's bitterest sorrow.

> *The proverbs of Solomon. A wise son maketh a glad father, but a foolish son is the heaviness of his mother* (Proverbs 10:1).

Only a mother who has suffered for raising a rebellious child can know the pain that words are inadequate to express. This is why I have dubbed the mother who insists on training her children according to her own immediate emotions as the "play-now-pay-later" mother.

The mother who learns to love her children Biblically may pay some emotional costs while they learn to live rightly. However, by paying those costs she will secure her children's future maturity, as well as her own peace of mind. She must learn to be a "pay-now-play-later" mom. The following is one woman's example that I hope will encourage the reader to love her children with a Titus 2:4 love.

A Mother's Struggle

A mother I know still recalls the emotional struggle that she had when her seventeen-year-old son decided to leave home. The family home was situated in a green valley surrounded by steep hills. It was a lovely home where meals were regular and many other comforts were freely provided for all the couple's children. Nevertheless, with only his clothes, bicycle, and a job at a fast-food restaurant, the self-confident and rebellious boy decided he could make his own way in the world. His salary barely afforded him the ability to pay for lunchmeat and rent. There was nothing left to buy such things as a used car for transportation.

One particularly cold winter day, the boy rode his bicycle from his apartment to the family home for a visit with his worried mother. After their visit, she watched him put on two sets of clothing and a knit hat over a ski mask before riding his bike to the apartment that he shared with two other young men. The wind was blowing icy sleet against him as he bent low in an attempt to ride his bicycle up a hill that even cars were struggling to climb. Her mother's heart bled because she wanted nothing more than to protect her son from such a difficult struggle – but she allowed him to struggle on alone. Why?

The reason she did nothing was because the boy had been acting rebelliously for several years prior to his leaving home. When he finally said he was definitely leaving home, her husband decided that it was time for him to learn the realities of life. Her motherly protectiveness was fearful for her son so she pleaded with her husband (in private) to forbid the boy to leave. However, the father knew the lessons that this particular boy needed to learn in order to become a responsible man. Furthermore, he knew it was best to learn those lessons early in life, rather than later. Although it hurt the father as much as it hurt the mother, he had enough long-ranged love for his son to let him go.

The mother's feelings of pain, fear, and protectiveness made it particularly difficult to refrain from babying her son in an attempt to make his chosen life easier. She knew she could buy him clothing, give him money, or sneak food to him without the father knowing. Graciously, the Lord had taught her to trust His design of submission to her husband and to trust Him with the lives of her loved ones. Therefore, as she watched her son ride into the icy wind that day, she prayed and entrusted him to God.

Several years (and many mother's prayers) later this same son emerged as a truly fine man. God had used the trials that he faced in his early manhood to teach him a strong work ethic. Even more important to his maturation was that he became a responsible adult who understood personal accountability for his own actions. When he was thirty years old he confessed that although he directed his rebellion towards his parents, he was truly in rebellion against God. It was not until God allowed many trials in his life that the boy's willfulness was broken and a man emerged. He also told his mother that the most meaningful thing in his childhood was that his parents put forth a united front. As a child he was not happy about it, but as an adult he appreciated that he was unable to play on his mother's emotions in order to escape his father's lessons.

To this day the young man's mother shudders to think of the willful, disrespectful man that he might have become if she had interfered with her husband's decision many years previously. She could have made his life easier when he was seventeen, but in so doing she might have been instrumental in preventing him from becoming a responsible adult. The times that she may have been correct in her assessment of her husband's child-training tactics were inconsequential compared to the rightness of living in God's design. Additionally, her interference could have been destructive to her relationship with her husband. Only God could bring everything together and ultimately make things right for the entire family.

Like this woman, you too can love your children according to a Titus 2:4 love. When a woman lives according to Biblical womanhood she is a living example of the power of trusting

God beyond what she can feel, see, or touch. God's omnipotence (all power), omnipresence (all presence), and omniscience (all knowledge) supports His design, and His love for her and her children are superior to the mere natural love of any human mother.

CHAPTER XXII

VULNERABILITY TO SUFFERING

The woman said, "Let me get this straight. You are saying that if I want to be a Biblical wife I must voluntarily give up my life and place my entire future in the hands of my husband? No way! I am not willing to be that vulnerable. My husband is not completely mature, he is not always trustworthy, and he has far less common sense than I do. I can think for myself and do not need anyone else telling me what to do. I am going to maintain control over my own life, thank you."

This hypothetical woman senses that if a wife follows her husband's lead he may lead her in a direction that will cause her to suffer. Her observations are absolutely correct. Men are capable of any conceivable sin or possible error. They can be inconsiderate and selfish or they can make unintentional mistakes, like becoming involved in a financial venture that fails.

Although her insight is humanly correct, this woman's belief that she can avoid suffering by maintaining personal control is spiritually very wrong. There are at least three errors in her reasoning that have led her to this incorrect conclusion. First, she assumes that only she is able to protect herself from unfair suffering. This woman's reasoning is flawed partly because no human being possesses enough power to protect them in the dangerous world in which we live. There are simply too many things that can happen over which a woman has no control at all. One only needs to observe the daily news to realize that we are constantly vulnerable to harm. Swirling around all of us are many unseen winds of danger that threaten our fragile human plans with tragedy. If a woman believes she has the ability to protect herself from suffering, she vastly overestimates her own power. Worse yet, she underestimates God's power to protect His own. Rejection of God's design never has and never will make a woman less susceptible to suffering. Help and protection from harm comes from the Lord to those who trust Him enough to live according to His ways.

> *Delight thyself also in the LORD; and he shall give thee the desires of thine heart. Commit thy way unto the LORD; trust also in him; and he shall bring it to pass* (Psalms 37:4-5).

> *Cast not away therefore your confidence, which hath great recompence of reward. For ye have need of patience, that, after ye have done the will of God, ye might receive the promise* (Hebrews 10:35-36).

The second flaw in the woman's reasoning is that she assumes she can reject God's design for womanhood and be allowed to escape any negative consequences. In reality, there is no better way to ensure suffering than to reject God's ways and to go one's own way.

> *Yea, they have chosen their own ways, and their soul delighteth in their abominations. I also will choose their delusions, and will bring their fears upon them; because when I called, none did*

*answer; when I spake, they did not hear: but
they did evil before mine eyes, and chose that in
which I delighted not* (Isaiah 66:3b-4).

This passage reveals that the one who goes her own way
will actually bring to pass her worst fears. For instance, I know
a woman whose husband was offered stock in his company at a
greatly discounted cost. However, this woman was intimidated
by her fear of loss and that fear motivated her into preventing
her husband from participating in his company's offer. The
result has been a loss of thousands of dollars that would have
secured a very comfortable retirement today. Hundreds of
examples of how a wife has interfered with her husband's
decision to begin a new business, or move in order to obtain a
better job, or to be more strict in the training of their children
could be given with the same type of disastrous results. Vastly
more Christians suffer from the misery they create for
themselves than those who follow God's plan.

The third flaw is the woman's assumption that suffering
unjustly is the worst thing that can happen and that it must be
avoided at all cost. Sadly, this assumption is more common in
the Christian community than one might realize. Christians
often fear that obeying God may cause them to suffer loss. Such
fear induces many people to ignore God's ways and to conform
to the world out of self-protection. For instance, fear of ridicule
may lead a Christian to cease witnessing for Christ; fear of
ostracism may entice a teen to follow the popular, but wrong
crowd; fear of losing business may tempt a man to be dishonest;
and fear of her husband's mistakes or possible maltreatment
may cause a woman to reject Biblical womanhood. A Christian
woman should not allow foreboding imaginations about what
terrible things might happen to tempt her from obeying God.
Just as God is able to award the business contract to the man
who will not be bribed, He is also able to bless the wife who
follows her husband's immature leadership. However, if God

does allow suffering in a woman's life, we can be sure that He has also provided a way for her to be blessed through that suffering.

There are so many positive things that God can reveal during the suffering of a Christian. If it were not so painful we might even look forward to it, rather than try to avoid it. Let us look at God's positive reasons for allowing suffering to enter a Christian's life.

The Positive Side of Suffering

1. It was necessary for Christ to suffer unjustly in order to provide us with a way of salvation.

> *For Christ also hath once suffered for sins, the just for the unjust, that he might bring us to God, being put to death in the flesh, but quickened by the Spirit* (1 Peter 3:18).

2. Christ suffered to fulfill God's plan, and to bring glory to Him. The unfair suffering in a Christian's life is for the same purpose.

> *But rejoice, inasmuch as ye are partakers of Christ's sufferings; that, when his glory shall be revealed, ye may be glad also with exceeding joy. If ye be reproached for the name of Christ, happy are ye; for the spirit of glory and of God resteth upon you: on their part he is evil spoken of, but on your part he is glorified* (1 Peter 4:13-14).

3. Christians should not be surprised when trials enter their lives.

> *Beloved, think it not strange concerning the fiery trial which is to try you, as though some strange thing happened unto you* (1 Peter 4:12).

4. Since Christians cannot expect to escape unfair suffering in this life, then suffering should be endured with the correct attitude.

> *For this is thankworthy, if a man for conscience toward God endure grief, suffering wrongfully. For what glory is it, if, when ye be buffeted for your faults, ye shall take it patiently? but If, when ye do well, and suffer for it, ye take it patiently, this is acceptable with God* (1 Peter 2:19-20).

> *For it is better, if the will of God be so, that ye suffer for well doing, than for evil doing* (1 Peter 3:17).

5. Satan uses temptations to persuade believers to fail God. However, the God of grace allows trials to present believers an opportunity to grow spiritually and to glorify Him.

> *Then Satan answered the LORD, and said, Doth Job fear God for nought? Hast not thou made an hedge about him, and about his house, and about all that he hath on every side? thou hast blessed the work of his hands, and his substance is increased in the land. But put forth thine hand now, and touch all that he hath, and he will curse thee to thy face (Job 1:9-11).*

> *But the God of all grace, who hath called us unto his eternal glory by Christ Jesus, after that ye have suffered a while, make you perfect, stablish, strengthen, settle you* (1 Peter 5:10).

6. God has a good purpose for the suffering He allows in a Christian's life. He desires for a believer to go through suffering and become strengthened by it. He does not want a Christian to run from suffering and remain spiritually weak.

*That the trial of your faith, being much more
precious than of gold that perisheth, though it
be tried with fire, might be found unto praise
and honour and glory at the appearing of Jesus
Christ* (1 Peter 1:7).

7. Suffering is not something of which to be ashamed.
Suffering can be the catalyst for spiritual growth in the life
of a believer, and it can be the means of spreading the love
of God to others. This is equally true when believers suffer
from problems in their marriages, as it is if they suffer from
any other hardship such as illness or financial loss.

*And not only so, but we glory in tribulations
also: knowing that tribulation worketh patience;
And patience, experience; and experience, hope:
And hope maketh not ashamed; because the love
of God is shed abroad in our hearts by the Holy
Ghost which is given unto us* (Romans 5:3-5).

8. From God's perspective, trials are not disasters but rather
opportunities to apply His power to real-life situations.

*In famine he shall redeem thee from death: and
in war from the power of the sword. Thou shalt
be hid from the scourge of the tongue: neither
shalt thou be afraid of destruction when it
cometh* (Job 5:20-21).

*There hath no temptation taken you but such as
is common to man: but God is faithful, who will
not suffer you to be tempted above that ye are
able; but will with the temptation also make a
way to escape, that ye may be able to bear it* (1
Corinthians 10:13).

9. Suffering teaches believers that worldly things are far less important than their relationship with Christ.

Not that I speak in respect of want: for I have learned, in whatsoever state I am, therewith to be content. I know both how to be abased, and I know how to abound: every where and in all things I am instructed both to be full and to be hungry, both to abound and to suffer need. I can do all things through Christ which strengtheneth me (Philippians 4:11-13).

10. Tribulations on earth are temporary and insignificant compared to the eternal values that trials can produce in the life of a believer.

For I reckon that the sufferings of this present time are not worthy to be compared with the glory which shall be revealed in us (Romans 8:18).

For our light affliction, which is but for a moment, worketh for us a far more exceeding and eternal weight of glory (2 Corinthians 4:17).

The verses above are only a portion of the many Scriptures that teach a Christian about the positive side of suffering. I highly recommend reading Joni Eareckson Tada's book, *Joni*, for a study of suffering. Suffering is something that Joni understands intimately. She has endured trials that make most of our problems appear insignificant by comparison. The principles in her book apply equally as well to minor marriage difficulties as they do to major tragedies. Also, you may wish to read my husband's book, *What the Bible Says About ... Suffering*, for an in-depth and systematic theological study on God's purpose for suffering.

In Conclusion

Yes, a woman places herself in a vulnerable position when she voluntarily submits herself to her husband's leadership. However, she becomes vulnerable not to a man, but to God's plan for her life. She also places herself in the best possible position to glorify God as she utilizes His power during any trials that may result from following Him.

A woman who lives according to Biblical truth may appear weak to some uninformed or misguided women, but actually she could never be stronger. The vulnerable woman can experience God's power in ways that those who renounce His design will never know or understand. If living Biblically opens a Christian up to ridicule and rejection from the world, then so be it. Such vulnerability simply allows God's power to shine through to all those who seek Him.

> *And he said unto me, My grace is sufficient for thee: for my strength is made perfect in weakness. Most gladly therefore will I rather glory in my infirmities, that the power of Christ may rest upon me. Therefore I take pleasure in infirmities, in reproaches, in necessities, in persecutions, in distresses for Christ's sake: for when I am weak, then am I strong*
> (2 Corinthians 12:9-10).

CHAPTER XXIII

FROM THE PAIN OF TRIBULATION
TO THE JOY OF THANKSGIVING

On a particularly beautiful morning Rick and I were sitting on our Arizona patio simply enjoying one another's company when the telephone rang. The caller was a young woman who had separated from her husband a few months earlier. I could hear the weariness in her voice as she asked, "What are you doing?" I replied, "Rick and I were just having our morning coffee outside on the patio." Sadly, she replied, "Oh, how nice. I wish my husband and I could have had companionship like that."

My mind flashed back over the more than thirty years that Rick and I had been married. I envisioned our years as a trip that began on the day we wed and will continue until one of us goes to meet the Lord in heaven. Rick and I have traveled a long and sometimes turbulent path together. There were plenty of sunny years, but there were also dark and stormy years where the dream of peaceful mornings on a patio would have seemed impossible. How I wanted to tell my young caller that Arizona mornings do not just happen. The path to such peaceful times is like a toll road. The fare to travel this road is persistent endurance through many years of both pain and pleasure. If a woman is not willing to pay the toll, she cannot acquire the type of long-term companionship that Rick and I have developed through the years. Such a companionship is built on common experiences and a binding commitment that is not abandoned during difficult times.

How did Rick and I arrive at our Arizona patio? The funny thing is that we did not want to live in Arizona – ever. Although we were positive that we were in the Lord's will by moving there, our feelings about doing so were similar to the Israelites when they said to Moses, "*...because there were no graves in Egypt, hast thou taken us away to die in the wilderness?*" *(Exodus 14:11b.)* Needless to say we sold our Texas home and many of our belongings, packed what we were able to keep, said farewell to all three of our adult children, and moved to the "wilderness" with heavy hearts.

Before moving to Arizona, Rick and I thought the desert was nothing but dry parched air, scorpions, unbearable heat, no water, land that could grow little but cactus, and unknown suffering. However, we soon discovered that the dry air and heat felt good to our aching joints (most of the time), and that nine to ten months of the year were extremely pleasant. As for the cactus and no water, God provided us with a home where we had orange, grapefruit, lemon, and fig trees, and a back yard adjoining a man-made lake. We even discovered that the desert was a beautiful place where the cactus bloomed in the spring and where dust particles in the upper atmosphere produced the most beautiful sunsets we had ever seen. We grew to love our home in Arizona more than any home we had ever had before. What God provided for us was proof that even when things look like your worst nightmare, the reality can be a peaceful blessing.

Arizona mornings (and now California mornings) have become standard for Rick and me, but it was not always so.

We were married when I was seventeen and he was eighteen. Not only were we young and immature, we were also unbelievers who were rebelling against our parents – not very solid ground on which to begin a marriage. You can probably imagine the troubles we got ourselves into during our early years of marriage. However, those troubles turned out to be for our benefit because they brought us to our knees and prepared us for the realization that we needed salvation through Jesus Christ.

Rick and I accepted Christ after ten years of marriage, three children, and many mistakes. Virtually from the beginning of our new birth in Christ, God started us on a crash course of learning His Word. While He was stripping us of our alien, human thinking and replacing it with His own, we tried to stay at least one step ahead of our children in order to train them in the Lord. It was not easy, but it was probably the happiest time of my life. I was excited about the Word of God and for the first time our lives had purpose. Little did I know that God was using those kindergarten years of learning His Word as a prelude to a test that would turn my world upside down.

My Personal Testing

During my naive years I did not fully realize that learning **about** the Bible and **living** it were two different things. During those years of Christian childhood, I could talk excitedly about the doctrine of absolute dependency on the Lord. However, my talk was as idle chatter because in reality I was depending more on my husband than I was on God. For my own good this unhealthy allegiance to a human being had to be reversed, and my dependency on God alone had to become total and complete. To this end, my loving Heavenly Father allowed certain events to occur where Rick was removed as my lifeline and God was "all" that I had left.

The exact details of the events that shook my foundation are of little importance, except to say that they caused shock, fear, humiliation, and extreme suffering for both my husband and myself. For a while Rick failed me, I failed him, and we both failed our God. There were times when the only correct thing we did was to hang in there, stay together, and keep returning to the Lord our God.

There really are no words for the pain that I felt during that terrible test. It was similar to having major surgery without anesthesia. There were long periods when I was in such turmoil that my chest hurt and I understood the meaning of heartache. I thought the lump in my throat would actually choke me. I cannot recount all the times that I felt rage and anger. Frequently I cried until there were no tears left and I heaved dry sobs. Once I was so desperate that I begged God to take me home so I could escape what I considered my prison of pain.

Does that shock you? Please do not let it. I am just a human being who relates to failure and the pain of suffering that is common to all of mankind. In fact, this book could not be written until after God took my crushed pride, shame, fear, weakness, and total failure to teach me His forgiveness. Without knowing His dependability, anything I might have written would have been just another academic study. I would never have had the confidence to say, "Yes, Biblical womanhood can be lived in this modern world!" This book is my unwavering testimony that God can transcend any human experience and that He is there for His suffering children when and if they turn to Him. It is my grateful song of joy for what God did and what He taught me through pain and suffering. Once, I only **said** that God's ways were best, but after experiencing Him repeatedly honoring His Word I now **know** that His plans are far superior to my own.

God first taught me His Word and then He gave me ample opportunity to apply His ways to real life. Through personal tribulation, and failure as well as some successes, He allowed me to learn many valuable lessons. In addition, I have learned a great deal from the suffering of others. The following are some of the lessons that I have gleaned through my years of study, experience, and observation. I have learned there are some very definite things to do and things not to do during suffering situations. Best of all I have been privileged to see God work through human pain. If my eyewitness account can help other women as they go through life's trials, then I have one more reason for praise and thanksgiving to God.

Advice from an Experienced Witness to Pain

1. Do not run away! There were many times I felt like giving up and running away. However, God does not want us to run from our problems. The greatest good comes into our lives when we allow Him to carry us through our troubles to His glory. Going through tribulation in marriage is a test of fire that is very painful, but when the pain is endured the final results can be better than whatever we had previously. Emotional love is kid's stuff compared to the love that passes through the test of fire and emerges stronger, purer, and better defined than ever before.

2. One of the most effective ways to have one's own character revealed and purified is during intense suffering. Trials have a way of revealing who we really are, both good and bad. During troubled times, such flaws as pride become evident and unknown strengths, like the ability to forgive and forget, can emerge.

3. God's plan is so complex that He can use a single trial and tailor it to meet the needs of every person involved. It is God's desire that every believer grows to be more Christ-like. However, the fire of adversity must refine each individual's character before she is a finished work. For one

person the trial may be chastisement for sin in her life, while for another the same adversity may be an opportunity to practice longsuffering and Christ-like forgiveness.

4. Trials often help to develop a true love. True love loves the unlovely, gives to the selfish, remains faithful to the unfaithful, and forgives the unforgivable – just as our Lord has forgiven us.

> *For if ye love them which love you, what thank have ye? for sinners also love those that love them. And if ye do good to them which do good to you, what thank have ye? for sinners also do even the same. And if ye lend to them of whom ye hope to receive, what thank have ye? for sinners also lend to sinners, to receive as much again. But love ye your enemies, and do good, and lend, hoping for nothing again; and your reward shall be great, and ye shall be the children of the Highest: for he is kind unto the unthankful and to the evil. Be ye therefore merciful, as your Father also is merciful*
> (Luke 6:32-36).

Prayer is Essential, Not Optional

1. I saw God work in my life more during my time of suffering than at any other time of my life. My prayers became regular and intense. I found that my mind was especially alert to His presence and my heart was more open to receive His love.

There are many advantages to prayer. When a woman is in open communication with God she is in the optimum position to see Him work beyond all human limitations. It is not that she will escape all fear and pain, but that she will learn to let God carry that fear and ease that pain.

2. Prayer has a calming effect on the soul and brings frustrations into perspective. It slows a woman's emotional reactions to problems and it increases her ability to mentally focus on solutions that are more Christ-like.

3. Serious trials cannot be overcome in the power of the flesh. If they must be endured, it must be in God's way and with His power. Consistent prayer, acknowledgement of personal sin, and commitment to being a *"doer of the work"* is a daily must.

> *For if any be a hearer of the word, and not a doer, he is like unto a man beholding his natural face in a glass: For he beholdeth himself, and goeth his way, and straightway forgetteth what manner of man he was. But whoso looketh into the perfect law of liberty, and continueth therein, he being not a forgetful hearer, but a doer of the work, this man shall be blessed in his deed* (James 1:23-25).

4. Do not be afraid to tell God exactly how you feel. Some people seem to believe that God only wants to hear pious prayers from people of sinless perfection. However, if you deny that such things as anger or bitterness exist within you, how can these negative feelings be dealt with properly? Certainly, the writer of Psalm 77 understood how to pour his true feelings out to God in prayer.

> *I cried unto God with my voice, even unto God with my voice; and he gave ear unto me. In the day of my trouble I sought the Lord: my sore ran in the night, and ceased not: my soul refused to be comforted. I remembered God, and was*

troubled: I complained, and my spirit was
overwhelmed. (Psalm 77:1-3).

5. Disclose every evil thought you have to God; He knows
anyway. During one of my most difficult times I remember
expressing my anger and frustration to God. I prayed
through tears and confessed that the emotional pain I was
feeling caused me to want to run away. However, no matter
how much I fumed, my tears eventually ceased and God
would remind me of His absolute power and goodness.

I will remember the works of the LORD: surely
I will remember thy wonders of old. I will
meditate also of all thy work, and talk of thy
doings. Thy way, O God, is in the sanctuary:
who is so great a God as our God? Thou art the
God that doest wonders: thou hast declared thy
strength among the people (Psalm 77:11-14).

After such "discussions" with God, He always granted me
the strength to continue on for just one more day.

6. Pray without ceasing. Pray for an end to your suffering,
but do so with a willingness to accept God's Will and His
perfect timing. Too often we make up our minds that what
we want is what God desires for us as well. Instead, be
prepared to accept His answer even before you know what
it is. For instance, a woman may be suffering because she
wants another child, but her husband does not. Because
she assumes that God's plan must be the same as her own,
she **tells** God to make her husband want to have a baby.
This woman is not praying for God's Will; she is dictating
to Him. When you go to God in prayer, do so with a desire
to discover and a willingness to accept His perfect Will – even
if your circumstances never change.

WARNING: Things to Avoid During Marriage Conflicts

1. The advice columnist, Ann Landers, often told a troubled wife to ask herself this question: "Would I be happier without my husband than I am with him?" This type of advice is humanistic, self-centered, and encourages the philosophy that one must live only for her own happiness and comfort. It also encourages running away from troubles and promotes the assumption that nothing will ever change for the better.

During marriage problems it is important to avoid thinking that the pain of today will last forever. Instead, with prayer and thanksgiving, ask God for His Will to be done and trust Him to bring it to pass.

2. Do not worry if you feel that you do not love your husband at the present time. When a woman is tired, discouraged, angry, or hurt, her thoughts tend to be very self-centered. In this state it is impossible to love someone else. It is also difficult to love emotionally the person who is causing you pain. Do not insist that your marriage is over if you, or even if your husband, does not presently "feel" in love. Get things right between yourself and God, concentrate on being a Biblical wife, exercise love, and in due time you can feel love again.

3. Be careful of your husband's reputation while talking to friends. Do not exaggerate his deficiencies, habits, moods, or occasional bad temper. Consider the effect of what you say to friends if they repeat or even further dramatize your husband's offenses. Even years after you and your husband have completely forgotten your disagreement, others may

still remember and continue to judge your husband for "mistreating" you.

4. There is nothing wrong with seeking advice from someone wiser and more experienced. However, do not talk indiscriminately with just anyone. "Helpful and loving" friends who take sides are not truly helpful. A woman should avoid anyone who fosters her feelings about being a suffering saint. Many divorces have been encouraged in this manner. Be especially wary of "support" groups where clusters of unhappy women "help" each other to justify their abandonment of God's design for womanhood. These groups often encourage a woman to defy her husband's leadership arrogantly, or they urge her to separate and finally to divorce him. If your advisors do not try to help you understand how God's design for womanhood applies to your particular problem, then beware of following their advice. Any advisor that you consult should have certain qualifications. First, the counselor should be a mature, Biblical Christian. Second, you need someone who will support you as you apply God's Word to your situation, not someone who will just agree with you. Your best choice of counselors would be a husband and wife team or an older woman from your church.

5. Be extra careful about being alone with another man (pastor, counselor, or friend). You are especially vulnerable to the attentions of a man when you are suffering emotionally. Furthermore, men can become exceedingly vulnerable to a damsel in distress. If you cry on a man's shoulder he may begin to feel protective toward you and you may respond to his attention with appreciation. Either of you could then misinterpret your feelings to be love. You could be starting something that should never be!

6. A woman's mind is similar to a video recorder that can tape memories. Whenever a woman suffers she tends to replay those recorded memories and relives every hurtful thing her husband has ever done or said. Playing with these mental images is a little like the old game of gossip. Each time the gossip is repeated the story is dramatized and embellished until it no longer resembles what actually took place. Such mental games actually create new pain as a woman's mind takes past events and projects them into the present. As memories of yesterday's pain are piled on top of new disappointments, the original events become distorted and the intensity of the present offense is multiplied. Women who have played these negative memory games for years wind up bitter and angry. In addition, they often become more than a little self-righteous as they demonize their husband's and justify their own part in the marriage problem.

Each time you remember something that emotionally hurts, refuse to play with it in your mind and turn to God in prayer instead. You might also read your Bible, replay good memories of your husband, do some exercise, talk to a cheerful friend, or almost anything that will divert your attention from your negative thoughts and feelings.

7. Avoid listening to sad music while you are suffering. Do not watch soap operas, daytime talk shows on television, or watch love-triangle movies that promote the idea that all men are evil and selfish creatures. Your emotions are already tender and such "entertainment" can only cause you to relate to other women's problems as if they were your own. One hour of this type of bonding with "other mistreated" women and you will be primed with self-righteous indignation and ready for battle the minute your husband walks through the door after work.

8. Be very careful about what you read. Reading romance novels (even Christian ones) promotes the development of romantic fantasies about men and marriage. No real man can live up to a romance novel's description of a sensitive and debonair Prince who sweeps a damsel off her feet and carries her to utopia.

In Conclusion

When a woman is suffering marriage problems, it is very difficult for her to accept that the best way to solve those problems is to continue to endure suffering. No one wants to hear such advice. It goes against the sin nature's tendency to fight for one's rights or to flee from pain. Although I empathize with the human desire to escape pain as quickly as possible, I also am aware that fight nor flight is seldom God's way to deal with the suffering that He allows in our lives. Instead, He desires for His children to be delivered from adversity by, and through, His power.

> *Ye shall not need to fight in this battle; set yourselves, stand ye still, and see the salvation of the Lord with you* ... (2 Chronicles 20:17a).

God always desires the best for His children. He wants a Christian woman to trust that He will carry her through any suffering that comes into her life. He wants Christians to bear up under the difficulties of life by exercising longsuffering love and by holding fast to an unshakeable trust in Him.

> *Charity suffereth long, and is kind; charity envieth not; charity vaunteth not itself, is not puffed up, Doth not behave itself unseemly, seeketh not her own, is not easily provoked, thinketh no evil; Rejoiceth not in iniquity, but rejoiceth in the truth; Beareth all things, believeth all things, hopeth all things, endureth all things* (1 Corinthians 13:4-7).

The woman who perseveres during trials will benefit from an enhanced spiritual life and an increased understanding of God's ultimate purposes for her life. This is of far greater value than would be a life lived without trials and suffering.

> *And beside this, giving all diligence, add to your faith virtue; and to virtue knowledge; And to knowledge temperance; and to temperance patience; and to patience godliness; And to godliness brotherly kindness; and to brotherly kindness charity. For if these things be in you, and abound, they make you that ye shall neither be barren nor unfruitful in the knowledge of our Lord Jesus Christ* (2 Peter 1:5-8).

The sweet victory of suffering occurs when the Christian's pain is turned to thanksgiving.

> *But thanks be to God, which giveth us the victory through our Lord Jesus Christ* (1 Corinthians 5:57).

Once when I was under such intense pressure that I could not concentrate long enough to pray silently, I would write my prayers. Writing letters to God seemed to help me express my thoughts better. Perhaps it will help other women who are presently suffering if I share one of those prayers.

A Prayer During Suffering

Heavenly Father, you know my heart is troubled. You know my weakness and my sorrows.

Father, remind me of your wisdom when I am in my own human thoughts.

Remind me of your sovereignty when I feel a loss of control.

Remind me of your grace and mercy when I am angry with others.

Remind me of your presence and loving care when I feel alone.

Grant me peace and calm during my troubles and help me to remember I am cradled in your everlasting love.

Give me your strength in order to withstand all that is happening and strength to endure the future.

Oh, how I thank you Father for your forgiveness for my sins. I know your hand is stretched out to all who turn to you and I thank you. I thank you ahead of time for answering this prayer.

In my soul I hold fast to your hand for guidance and for a steady foot as I walk through my valley of pain and tears.

Even though I often falter Father, I pray that you will still be glorified and that ultimately your will is done in my life.

I thank you for the peace of knowing that you have all things in control and that you will always do what is best for everyone concerned. In Jesus name, Amen.

This prayer was answered in every way! Now, with the Psalmist my "mourning has turned into dancing" and I am gratefully able to give thanks to God for my suffering.

Thou hast turned for me my mourning into dancing: thou hast put off my sackcloth, and girded me with gladness; To the end that my glory may sing praise to thee, and not be silent. O LORD my God, I will give thanks unto thee for ever (Psalm 30:11-12).

CHAPTER XXIV

HELP! I HAVE DONE EVERYTHING WRONG!

This chapter is for the woman who feels she is without hope. She may believe that she has failed God so completely that recovery is impossible. She may be divorced and is buried with a crushing sense of guilt for her role in the breakup of her marriage. She may now realize that she might have made her marriage work if she had only understood Biblical womanhood years earlier. Or, she may recognize that her present marriage problems are due largely to her own violation of God's design for womanhood. However, nothing is impossible with God. No matter what our failures in the past may be, our future can be filled with hope and redemption.

Our God is a God of restoration and stability. As long as there remains a breath of life in us there is no such thing as a lost cause. If there were truly a hopeless case I imagine Paul would have been one. Before his conversion, he consented to the stoning of Stephen (Acts 7:58-8:1) and he enthusiastically persecuted the early church. What Paul did to the early Christians was probably the reason that he called himself "chief" among sinners in 1 Timothy 1:15. He might have carried a tremendous sense of guilt and shame forever if he had not understood the abundant grace and forgiveness of our Heavenly Father.

> *But where sin abounded, grace did much more*
> *abound: That as sin hath reigned unto death,*
> *even so might grace reign through righteousness*
> *unto eternal life by Jesus Christ our Lord*
> (Romans 5:20b-21).

Paul is not the only one who has been forgiven shameful sins. Many sinners (myself included) have found victory over past offences through God's grace. Hebrews 11 provides a comforting historical record of His forgiveness of other sinful humans. These people failed in diverse ways (everything from prostitution to murder) but they each succeeded in at least one important way. All of them conquered their impossible situations by placing their complete trust in God. They then placed their past behind them and allowed Him to direct their future lives. Their names have been recorded in the Bible for our benefit. They are examples to all mankind that God forgives and even promotes any who will turn to Him.

As it was for the people in Hebrews 11, so it is for a Christian woman today. Most of the Hebrews 11 people failed God at some point in their lives, but they went on to serve Him. Likewise, God's plan for a modern woman's life is not terminated by her past or present failures. Instead, her future is dependent solely on whether she will entrust herself to the abundant grace of God today, and everyday from this point on. The following are three essential steps in correctly entrusting oneself to the grace of God.

Entrusting Yourself to the Grace of God

Step One: A Prayer of Confession – An admission of wrongdoing (the acceptance of personal accountability).

*If we confess our sins, he is faithful and just to
forgive us our sins, and to cleanse us from all
unrighteousness* (1 John 1:9).

Personal acknowledgement of wrongdoing is always the
first step when we become aware that we have sinned against
God. This includes adultery, divorce, lack of submission,
or any other sin. When we acknowledge our transgressions
to God we are forgiven for all our known and even our
unknown sins. His forgiveness cleanses us and makes us
pure before God. Our sin is wiped from the slate. This
prepares us for the second step in surrendering our present
and future to God.

Step Two: Forgiving One's Self.
The following is a saying that my husband wrote. It means
so much to me that I have posted it on my office wall.
"If you find yourself dwelling on the mistakes
of the past, it is because you are not living your
potential in the present. When you are not living
your potential for today, the mistakes of the past
become unbearable."

Rick wrote this profound statement one day when he realized
that he was allowing his mind to dwell on the sins of his
past. He became conscious of the fact that his thoughts
were causing him to make the past more real than his present.
With the past clouding his mind he was unable to appreciate
his present life. By allowing himself to forget God's grace,
he was also triggering a sense of guilt that hampered his
ability to accomplish his current mission in life. This was a
turning point in my dear husband's life. He realized that
when God forgives, He forgives completely. Realizing this,
Rick was finally able to also forgive himself. Like my

husband, before you can move forward in your life, you
must accept God's forgiveness and forgive yourself as well.

> *... but this one thing I do, forgetting those things*
> *which are behind, and reaching forth unto those*
> *things which are before, I press toward the mark*
> *for the prize of the high calling of God in Christ*
> *Jesus* (Philippians 3:13b-14).

Step Three: A Total Commitment and Surrender to God's
Ways

> *Then said Jesus unto his disciples, If any man*
> *will come after me, let him deny himself, and*
> *take up his cross, and follow me*
> (Matthew 16:24).

> *I beseech you therefore, brethren, by the mercies*
> *of God, that ye present your bodies a living*
> *sacrifice, holy, acceptable unto God, which is*
> *your reasonable service* (Romans 12:1).

This third step is often omitted when people speak only of
the grace of God. Some believers wrongly assume that since
grace abounds and covers all past sins that a Christian can
continue to disobey God's design for womanhood and
marriage. Not so!

> *What shall we say then? Shall we continue in*
> *sin, that grace may abound? God forbid. How*
> *shall we, that are dead to sin, live any longer*
> *therein?* (Romans 6:1-2).

God forbid that a Christian should knowingly and willfully
continue in any disobedience of God! Arrogantly taking
advantage of God's grace is not the same as entrusting
oneself to His grace. God wipes out our past failures upon

our confession of those sins. He even delivers His humble children from our present deficiencies, but His grace is not a license for us to sin deliberately.

A Closing Message for You

Is it possible for you to live womanhood in today's world? Yes, you can! You can because your ability to live Biblically does not depend on your past or your present circumstances. It does not depend on your perfection; but instead, it depends entirely on God's perfection. God has designed a specific purpose for a woman, He has commanded a believing woman to live according to that design, and if she will just call upon Him He will empower her to accomplish His goal for her life.

> *And God is able to make all grace abound toward you; that ye, always having all sufficiency in all things, may abound to every good work:* (2 Corinthians 9:8).

Today can be the first day of your new life! You can move forward from this point on and know:

1. That God loves you,

2. That He has forgiven you for all your past sins, and

3. That you can trust Him to be with you as you obey His design for womanhood today and in the future.

If you are presently having marriage problems, simply begin today to live according to principles. Trust God to enable you to become a Biblical wife. If you are separated or divorced from your husband, and neither of you have remarried, pray that God will make it possible for you to be reconciled. Approach your husband with what you have learned and ask for his forgiveness for the part that you played in your separation.

If you are divorced and have no possibility for reconciliation because of remarriage, then forgive yourself (and your ex-husband) and trust God for your future. If you are remarried, then begin today to make your present marriage a one. Whatever your present circumstances, no matter how black or how bright your future appears to you, commit your life to God. Begin living womanhood today and rejoice as He works to bring about His will in your life.

> *So shall my word be that goeth forth out of my*
> *mouth: it shall not return unto me void, but it*
> *shall accomplish that which I please, and it shall*
> *prosper in the thing whereto I sent it*
> (Isaiah 55:11).

Some women may remain hesitant to take the first step of committing themselves to living Biblical womanhood. If this is true for you, you will need to reread this entire book prayerfully with a highlighter in one hand and your Bible in the other. In fact, no matter what your circumstances are today, you may need to reread it once a year as you and your marriage mature. In the meantime, keep the book handy for those specialized times when you need to refresh your memory. With each review, you will gain a deeper understanding of how to apply Biblical womanhood to your own life. On the following page is a topical list to aid you in reviewing specific subjects.

REVIEW LIST

1. For a better understanding of your husband's drive to lead, provide, and protect his family, review **Chapters II** through **IV, VII, VIII,** and **XIV** through **XVII**. Also, see *What the Bible Says About ... Being a Man*, by J. Richard Fugate, Foundation for Biblical Research, ISBN 1-889700-29-0.

2. For a better understanding of why you need your husband's authority and leadership, review: **Chapters III, IV,** and **V**.

3. For a better understanding of God's design for womanhood, review: **Chapters II** through **IV, VI, VIII** through **X,** and **XVI** through **XXI**.

4. For a better understanding of the difference between submission and obedience, review: **Chapter VI**.

5. For a better understanding of the powerful influence you have on your husband, review: Chapters **VII** through **IX**.

6. For a better understanding of how to communicate with your husband, review: **Chapters XIV** and **XV**.

7. For recognizing and defusing the influence of Satan in your life, review: **Chapters XII** and **XIII**.

8. For understanding why pain and tribulation cannot be completely avoided in your life, review: **Chapters XXII** and **XXIII**.

9. For a better understanding how to deal with your husband if he does not appear to be cooperating with your efforts to build a marriage, review: **Chapters XIV** through **XVI**.

10. For patience in holding fast to hope for a better tomorrow, review: **Chapters I, XXII**, and **XXIII**.

11. For a book you might recommend to your husband so he can better understand you and his own role, see: *What the Bible Says About...Being a Man*, by J. Richard Fugate, ISBN 1-889700-29-0.

And now, dear sisters in Christ, I trust my God to shower His abundant grace upon each of you as you commit yourself to living according to His design for Biblical womanhood. May He be glorified by your submission to His design.

> *Now the God of hope fill you with all joy and*
> *peace in believing, that ye may abound in hope,*
> *through the power of the Holy Ghost*
> (Romans 15:13).

> *To God only wise, be glory through Jesus Christ*
> *for ever. Amen* (Romans 16:27).

APPENDIX

Appendix

WOMEN ALONE

Marriage is a God-ordained institution that is meant to provide order in the family for men and women while they live upon this earth. There is no marriage in heaven.

> *For in the resurrection they neither marry, nor*
> *are given in marriage, but are as the angels of*
> *God in heaven* (Matthew 22:30).

Neither, a woman's salvation, her ability to live a Christian way of life, nor her Christian maturity is dependent on her ever being married. Some women are called by God to remain unmarried. Paul said that singleness is a specialized gift from God for certain people.

> *For I would that all men were even as I myself.*
> *But every man hath his proper gift of God, one*
> *after this manner, and another after that. I say*
> *therefore to the unmarried and widows, It is*
> *good for them if they abide even as I*
> (1 Corinthians 7:7-8).

There are two categories of single women. There are the women who have never been married and those who are widowed or divorced. In either category a woman has certain responsibilities, privileges, and restrictions for living as a Biblical woman. You will notice that most of the scriptural information concerning singleness has been taken from the Old Testament. This is because the Old Testament is where God first recorded the laws for all human institutions.

The Woman Who Has Never Been Married

God provides for the unmarried girl through His institution – the family. He intends for a young woman to remain under the authority of her father until she marries (Numbers 30:3-5). And, she should not marry without her father's permission (1 Corinthians 7:36-38).

The responsibilities of an unmarried daughter include:

1. To honor and obey her parents (Exodus 20:12; 21:15, 17; Deuteronomy 5:16; 27:16; and Ephesians 6:2).

2. To learn the Word of God (Deuteronomy 29:18 & 29).

3. To not shame herself or her father by being promiscuous (Leviticus 21:9).

Her privileges include:

1. Protection and provision under her father's leadership. (Numbers 30:16; 2 Samuel 12:3; and Job 42:15).

2. An orphaned woman may receive the leadership and provisional care of her nearest relative (brother, uncle, etc.). (The book of Ruth and Esther 2:7). God, Himself, acts as her father if there are no male relatives to guide the unmarried woman (Psalm 68:5).

3. A single woman has the privilege of being less encumbered with the cares of this world than her married sister (1 Corinthians 7:28). An unmarried woman has more time to develop her personal relationship with Christ (1 Corinthians 7:34).

Her restrictions include:

1. She is restricted from making vows that do not have her father's approval. Her father's authority extends to reversal of any vows that she might make (Numbers 30:3-5).

2. She is to remain chaste (Deuteronomy 22:21; 1 Thessalonians 4:3-5).

The Widow and the Divorced Woman

In today's world we have many women who are either widowed or divorced. A woman in either of these conditions also has responsibilities, privileges, and restrictions. First, she is personally responsible to God for any vows that she makes (Numbers 30:9).

Her privileges include:

1. A right to receive care from her relatives (Leviticus 22:13; 1 Timothy 5:4 & 8).

2. Widows may also receive care from the church (1 Timothy 5:5-9).

3. A previously married woman no longer has a husband to protect her, but God will act as her husband and He will be as a father to her children (Psalms 10:14; 10:18; 68:5; and 82:3).

Her restrictions include:

1. If a Christian widow remarries it should be only to a fellow believer (1 Corinthians 7:39; 2 Corinthians 6:14).

2. A divorcee is restricted from remarriage for at least as long as her former husband is alive and reconciliation remains viable (1Corinthians 7:10-11; 7:13-16; and 7:27).

Advice for the Unmarried Woman

The material in this book is directed primarily to the married woman, however, if you are single you can still benefit by reading it in its entirety. This book contains information that will help you in the following areas:

1. Being aware that your design and purpose is very different from a man's.

2. Becoming more knowledgeable concerning your responsibilities, should you marry in the future.

3. Understanding what it means to remain a single woman. A woman does not leave her femininity at the door just because she is not married. For instance, you will not have to follow the leadership of a husband, but a better understanding of God's design for womanhood and manhood will help you treat all men with the proper respect and appreciation, and in return to solicit the proper respect for yourself. Understanding God's design for womanhood will also help you choose an appropriate occupation or ministry. Furthermore, knowledge of Biblical womanhood may help you to avoid those who would corrupt your mind, body, and spirit.

4. Considering the Biblical eligibility of any man who wishes to court you. (The only reason for a man and a woman to spend time together alone is to determine if they should marry.) As a single woman you have more choice than your married sister who reads this book **after** she is already married. You have the opportunity of gaining some valuable information before you make any marriage commitment.

Do not consider giving up your single life until you have read this entire book. After which, you will be better prepared to answer the following questions before you say, "I do."

1. Am I committed to honoring God's design for womanhood?

2. Do I know the intended man's family well? Do his father **and** mother treat each other in a Biblical manner and are their standards compatible with my own?

3. Does my father approve of this man and his family? (If your father is not alive or in some way unavailable, an elder brother or a church elder could be consulted.)

4. Is the man committed to God's will for his life?

5. Does he consider his Biblical responsibilities in marriage to be important?

6. Does he desire to provide for a family or does he want a financial partnership?

7. Does he take his responsibility as the spiritual leader of a family seriously?

8. Are his standards and way of life compatible with your own?

9. Am I willing to accept him as he is or, do I want to change something about him? Be Forewarned! Women who think they can change their men after they marry are in for a big surprise. Whatever you presently see is what you get – it may never change and is even likely to get worse.

10. Is he considerate, tender, and protective toward you in the way he speaks and acts? Does he consider your safety before he takes you somewhere?

11. Does he exhibit clear leadership that you can follow?

12. Does he desire to lead a wife or does he appear to want a mother to serve and lead him?

13. Are you willing to love, respect, and submit to him in a Biblical manner? Are you ready to trust this man with your body, mind, and emotions?

Some women panic if they are not married before they are thirty or forty. However, a woman is much better off remaining unwed until (or unless) God brings a godly man into her life. The key to happiness in life (married or single) is to be content in whatever state that you find yourself.

...for I have learned, in whatsoever state I am,
therewith to be content (Philippians 4:11b.)

May God reveal His plan for your life. May He bless and guide you in a life devoted to Him – married or single.

NOTES

1. Jess Stein, ed., *The Random House College Dictionary*, (rev. ed.; NY: Random House, 1975) p. 615. s.v. "helper" and its synonyms.

2. John Piper and Wayne Grudem, eds., *Recovering Biblical Manhood and Womanhood*, (Wheaton, Illinois: Crossway Books, a division of Good News Publishers, 1991), pp. 108, 109.

3. *The Compact Edition of the Oxford English Dictionary*, (Oxford: Oxford University Press, 1971), p. 143, s.v. "authority."

4. J. Richard Fugate, *What the Bible Says About...Child Training*, (Citrus Heights, CA: Foundation for Biblical Research, 1996), p. 38. Hebrew, '*elyon*, "high, supreme' from the verb '*alah*, "go up, ascend."

5. ibid., p. 38. Greek, *exousia* "authority;" those who are in a position of authority "officials, governments" (Romans 13:2; Luke 12:11; Titus 3:1).

6. ibid., p. 38 Greek, *tasso* "arrange, put in a place;" here referring to the authorities "instituted" (or arranged) by God.

7. *Obedience*, (The Foundation for Biblical Research, Citrus Heights, CA 1981). A theological study of God's institutions.

8. Ibid., *Submission*.

9. For a more in depth study of the woman's natural tendencies, read *Gender Sanity*, edited by Nicolas Davidson, (Lanham, MD: University Press of America, 1989).

10. Jess Stein, ed,. *The Random House College Dictionary*, (rev. ed.; NY: Random House, 1975), p. 422, s.v. "ego."

11. *Arizona Republic*, January 27, 1990, p. C-2.

12. Paul Kurtz, "Fulfilling Feminist Ideals: A New Agenda," *Free Inquiry*, Fall 1990, p. 21, as cited in *Understanding the Times*, David A. Noebel, (Manitou Springs, CO: Summit Press, 1991), p. 436.

13. Julian Huxley, *The Best of Humanism*, ed. Roger E. Greeley, 1945, (Buffalo: Prometheus, 1988), as cited in *Understanding the Times*, p. 116.

14. Elizabeth Cady Stanton, *Eighty Years and More,* 1998, as cited in *The Harper Book of American Quotations*, Gorton Carruth & Eugene Ehrich, (N.Y. Harper & Row, Publishers, IN. 1988, p. 495.

15. Annie Laurie Gaylor, "Feminist 'Salvation,'" *The Humanist*, July/August, 1988, p. 37, as cited in *Understanding the Times*, p. 486.

16. Gloria Steinem, *Outrageous Acts and Everyday Rebellions*, (Hinsdale, IL: Holt, Rinehart and Winston, 1983), p. 283.

17. Gloria Steinem, as cited in *Peter's Quotations: Ideas For Our Time*, Dr. Lawrence J. Peter, (New York: Bantam Books, 1977), as cited in *Never Too Early*, Doreen Claggett, (Melbourne, Florida, Dove Christian Books, 1989), p. 142.

18. Sol Gorden, "The Egalitarian Family is Alive and Well," *The Humanist*, May/June, 1975, p. 18, as cited in *Understanding the Times*, p. 436.

19. Dr. Joyce Brothers, "Why Wives Have Affairs," *Arizona Republic*, February 19, 1990, Parade section, p. 5.

20. Lynne Smith and Bob Sipchen "Most Parents Would Give Up Careers, Poll Says," *Arizona Republic*, August 12, 1990, p. A-1. The "Los Angeles Times" of 1,000 households in southern California's Los Angeles and Orange counties commissioned this survey.

21. Barry Lester, Ph.D., professor of psychiatry and pediatrics at Brown University and Bradley Hospital in Providence, Rhode Island discusses communication between mother and child as cited by Susan Goodman, "Presumed Innocents," *Modern Maturity* magazine, 1992, December/January, p. 27.

You may order additional copies of this book, *On the Other Side of the Garden*, ISBN 1-889700-40-1 ($11.95), as well as the Fugate's other titles by writing or calling:

Family Ministries,
PO Box 1412
Fair Oaks, CA 95628
Order Line: 1-800-545-1729

On the Other Side of the Garden – Study Workbook
by Romona Tuma – revised by Virginia Fugate
ISBN 1-889700-49-5 ($14.95)

On the Other Side of the Garden is being used by hundreds of womanhood classes around the country with miraculous results. Feminists are being converted to Biblical womanhood and women who believed they were already living Biblically are being challenged. Even couples' classes have produced positive results for both women and men. The workbook is a helpful tool for groups or individuals. It is also excellent for a mother and teenage daughter study.

Victorious Women
On the Other Side of the Garden
by Virginia Ruth Fugate
ISBN 1-889700-25-8 ($10.95)

Virginia invites you to join her on a heartwarming journey through a garden of other women's victories as she shares insights into Biblical womanhood. Where *On the Other Side of the Garden* presents the principles; *Victorious Women* shares real life examples of Biblical womanhood in action. The friendly format provides an easy atmosphere in which the stories of real women will encourage you also to overcome the challenges of being a woman in today's world. *On the Other Side of the Garden* is mind changing; *Victorious Women* will encourage your heart!

What the Bible Says About ... Being a Man
by J. Richard Fugate
ISBN 1-889700-29-0 ($11.95)

What this nation needs today are a few good men – men who will live by the Biblical principles of honesty, courage, loyalty, self-discipline, and above all, godliness. Over the past century, men have lost their vision for manhood. As a result parenting, marriage, government, business, and church have all suffered. *Being a Man* explains the Biblical roles of Christian masculinity and the road back to responsible manhood. This book is for any Christian man who would like to be a mature leader.

What the Bible Says About...Child Training
by J. Richard Fugate
ISBN 1-889700-13-4 ($12.95)

This book is considered by many to be the deepest and most comprehensive work on Biblical child training ever written. It has been accepted by thousands of Bible-believing churches as the standard text on child training for more than twenty-five years.

The unique aspect of *What the Bible Says About ... Child Training* is that the author accepts the Bible as absolute truth and infinitely superior to any human system of thinking. The system of child training presented has been used by over 300,000 families with dramatic results, thus providing the proof that testifies of all truth – IT WORKS!

What the Bible Says About ... Suffering
By J. Richard Fugate
ISBN 1-889700-35-5 ($12.00)

This book enables unbelievers to understand why God allows man to suffer and Christians to see how suffering is used for their spiritual growth. A great evangelical tool!

"J. Richard Fugate bases his discussion upon what the Bible says. He proffers a systematic theology on suffering to replace psychological programs found in modern counseling. The first section addresses both the Christian and non-Christian. It includes a well thought out explanation to the question: "Why does mankind suffer?" His analysis is Biblical, theologically sound, and logical. I highly recommend this book to begin a study of suffering from God's point of view."

Dr. John C. Beck, Jr., Professor of Theology
Chafer Theological Seminary, Orange County

Inquires for quantity discounts are welcomed at: cbg@rfugate.org
or call (916) 729-6993 for quotes.